Dawn Mattera has written a love letter to life. Through the lens of her travels to Italy and growing up in an Italian-American neighborhood, Dawn introduces us to a cast of characters. She shares her life lessons with enchanting storytelling, passion, wisdom and wit. Carpe Diem! Read this book PRONTO!

   —Lin Tucci, Two-Time SAG Award-Winning Actor

Weaving together Italian principles for a fulfilling life and her experiences, Dawn presents a plan for a Renaissance in your life. Through practical tips that feel achievable and a cheerful, down-to-earth attitude, she will guide and inspire you to create a life filled with passion, love, and hope.

   —Silvia Donati, Contributing Editor at *Italy Magazine*

Dawn Mattera is providing a path for others to improve their well-being by incorporating the Italian culture into their lives. Dawn's infectious enthusiasm to impart the Italian secrets of happiness she has learned through her lifelong association with Italian culture will inspire you to adopt them as well.

   —Matteo Platania, Co-founder
   mi.o – modern Italian network

THE ITALIAN ART OF LIVING

Your Passport to Hope, Happiness and Your Personal Renaissance

Dawn Mattera

AUTHOR ACADEMY elite

The Italian Art of Living
Your Passport to Hope, Happiness and Your Personal Renaissance
© Dawn Mattera
All rights reserved

Printed in the United States of America

Published by Author Academy Elite
P.O. Box 43, Powell, OH 43035
AuthorAcademyElite.com

Paperback: 978-1-64746-483-7
Hardback: 978-1-64746-484-4
Ebook: 978-1-64746-485-1

Library of Congress Control Number: 2020916760
Although the author and publisher have made every effort to ensure that the information in this book was correct at press time, the author and publisher do not assume and hereby disclaim any liability to any party for any loss, damage or disruption caused by errors or omission, whether such errors or omissions result from negligence, accident, or any other cause.

Disclaimer
The stories in this book have been documented to the best of the author's memory. Some names and identifying details have been changed to protect privacy.

Dedication

Without my grandparents' courage, faith and determination to build a life and legacy in America, I would not be who I am today. I am forever grateful to them, and will do my part to continue what they started.

My dearest friends are my extended family, offering love, encouragement and—when I need it—correction shared with compassion.

My *amore*, Bob, has loved, defended and supported me from the first day we met. I look forward to many more adventures together!

Most of all, I dedicate this book to God. My prayer is to share the grace, love and hope that I've been given.

TABLE OF CONTENTS

INTRODUCTION
LA DOLCE VITA (THE SWEET LIFE) IS POSSIBLE

"What the f*ck?!"

That's sometimes what I hear when I arrive home from the office. Thankfully, it's not directed at me! My partner, Bob, gets out of work an hour before I do. By the time I come home, he's been watching that train wreck of broadcasting known as the news. Have you noticed that there's rarely a happy story? Bob's outburst is one of frustration, disbelief and sometimes anger.

Every day, stories of destruction, suffering and catastrophe bombard us. Do you ever feel like our world is doomed? Do you think that you're helpless to do something about it? If so, I want to stamp your metaphorical passport and take you from a place of fear and apathy to a future of hope and enthusiasm.

Growing up in an Italian-American household and neighborhood taught me how to navigate through the storms of life. At the time, I didn't know that I was a student. Back then, we learned the lessons while sitting around the dinner table or through chats with the neighbors. We watched our parents and grandparents sort through difficulties, identify what was important, and build a community. Traveling to—and living in—Italy has shown me a resilient spirit of love, loyalty, creativity and perseverance. I'll now pass these lessons on to you, often with humor, sometimes with tough love, and always with compassion.

Further, we'll put your past in perspective, which will inspire you to move forward with confidence. In turn, you'll feel more equipped to bring your family and friends along for the adventure and encourage them to seek their own.

No matter your ethnic background, you can implement the ideas shared in this "guidebook" to create your Renaissance. You may also be surprised as we go beyond the stereotypes of just pasta, mobsters, and leaning towers.

You may not find the cure for cancer or become a world leader, but you can make a difference in the lives of those around you. You're a unique piece of the puzzle of life! If enough of us live up to our true potentials—in our little circles of influence—we can change the world!

Everything you live through helps to make
you the person you are now.

—Sophia Loren

CHAPTER 1
INSOMMA... (SO...)

CHALLENGES ARE A MATTER OF PERSPECTIVE

We spent over three hours on a crowded, stuffy and rickety train, going from Orvieto to Naples, Italy. We looked like our passport photos, and that's pretty scary! Then, we had a hair-raising taxi ride to the port followed by an hour on a boat. We finally arrived at the vibrant and welcoming home of my ancestors, the island of Ischia.

That evening, we talked—well, more accurately, whined—about how long it took to travel that day. A family member pointed out that we *chose* to take that route. *Insomma* (so), we shouldn't complain.

That's how I've seen many Italians look at problems. We always have a choice, even if it's not ideal or what we'd like. Do you hate your job? You are not chained to your desk. Are you frustrated with your weight? No one is force-feeding you. (That one is for me, too!)

Some of you may be tempted to stop reading this book right here. That's because you're looking for more than what you've already read elsewhere. You want answers for more painful issues like depression and heartbreak. Rest assured, my fellow traveler in life, that we'll tackle those topics in other chapters. For now, let's ease into improving our lives. After all, Rome wasn't built in a day.

No matter how severe the difficulty, we choose to become bitter or better—to be a victim or a victor. As a bitter victim, we feel trapped; as a better victor, we feel empowered and optimistic.

Events can blindside us, friends and lovers may betray us, we could get laid off a few years shy of retirement, or a hurricane could destroy our homes. Life is not always fair, but how you react during hard times is entirely up to you.

When the world stopped in its tracks in 2020, Italy was one of the hardest-hit nations. Instead of hoarding meat and hand sanitizer, Italians sang together from their balconies and watched movies projected onto the sides of buildings. They were the embodiment of the proverb that says, "As long as there is life, there is hope."

Although everyone needs a different amount of time to process something traumatic, I encourage you *not* to wait. Why? Because a highly-charged emotion can become our basic personality if we don't address it. Let me explain. You get some bad news and you're devastated. While there's nothing wrong with feeling a certain way, hanging on to that emotion can become a habit that eventually becomes an undesirable lifestyle.

I think about an acquaintance who, since her brother passed away decades ago, became irritable and grew mad at the world. She felt somewhat responsible for her brother's death because she didn't alert the doctors to a symptom. She was angry, mostly at herself.

By rehearsing the anger day after day, it became her habitual mood, which eventually changed her personality. Over time, she alienated her friends and family, which left her lonely and forgotten in her twilight years. This is a sad example of how a tragic event can scar us for life if we allow it.

To give you a more positive example, my grandmother spent the last ten years of her life in a wheelchair. Before the broken hip, she loved to spend time in her flourishing garden, attended church every Sunday, and visited family and friends.

Back in the 1970's, it wasn't easy for a person in a wheelchair to go anywhere. Even though my grandmother couldn't do most of the things that brought her joy, she still did what was most important to her—she showed love to her family and friends, mostly by cooking and baking for us!

My grandmother stayed socially connected by phone, and she watched church services on TV. She continued to can the vegetables that Grandpa picked from their garden. She never complained.

As my father always said to us—and his parents said to him— "Life goes on." We decide how we go on—we accept what we cannot change and making the most of what we have. When life gives us lemons, we make *limoncello*!

Think of your brain as a computer. Your repetitive thoughts become hard-wired programs. I'm sure that you want software that directs you to be enthusiastic rather than indifferent. We'll discuss this further in the chapter about habits. Here's a sneak preview: you can reprogram and reboot your brain.

Why do we even go through challenges, especially if we're the good guys? For some, it's the only way to learn empathy. For all of us, it deepens our compassion if we recognize it. We can help others because we relate to what they're facing. As we extend a hand, they feel connected rather than alone. This, in turn, strengthens our bonds with each other.

HOPE IS ALWAYS BETTER THAN DOUBT.

Take that idea a step further. Imagine if each of us reached out to another wounded soul. Wouldn't our families, communities, and perhaps even our world be a better place? Maybe I'm a dreamer, but hope is always better than doubt.

I can almost hear some readers snickering at my Pollyanna attitude. They'd point out that people—self-centered creatures that we are—can often be unkind. It reminds me of something I read years ago that puts this in perspective. When another person hurts us, it's a reminder that the only one we can ever trust all the time is God. We're human, which means we make mistakes and mistreat those we love. People disappoint us, and we do the same. For those who believe in a higher power, we can take comfort knowing there is One who'll never let us down.

I asked my dear friend, Colonel Frank Romano (Ret.), how he faces tragedy. Frank is a veteran of World War II, the Korean War, and the Vietnam War. He told me the story of when he was in command at the DMZ between North and South Korea, and tensions were high.

As Frank encouraged his men to stay strong and have faith, the Army chaplain asked Frank about his beliefs. It was a wake-up call because he'd drifted away from what was once a great resource in his life. Frank renewed his commitment to his faith and remains steadfast.

Being on Earth for 90+ years, Frank has witnessed many tragedies; his convictions are what carried him through them. Perhaps it's time for you to renew or find your beliefs for the first time. Will life be problem free? Um, no. But you may find a sense of peace and hope to make the journey easier.

Difficult times are also a stark reminder of all the good things we do have. You may have heard the parable of the two wolves fighting inside us. One is filled with lies, regret and resentment. The other is filled with truth, hope, and gratitude. Which wolf wins? The one you feed the most.

Focusing on the blessings in your life doesn't mean burying your head in the sand. The problems need to be solved, and we feel more empowered when we see that our assets greatly outweigh any liabilities. If we fixate on the difficulty, we keep hurting; if we learn from it, we keep growing.

When the situation doesn't go as we hoped, we certainly don't want to hear, "Maybe it's for the best." However, please consider that it might be. For example, I was crushed and embarrassed when I got divorced. Even though I was unhappy, I'd made a vow. Further, I was afraid that I'd be lonely as a single, post-middle-aged woman. Yet, I did go on to meet someone who became the love of my life. If I'd moped around, fixated only on the hurt and despair, I would've missed meeting Mr. Right. (By the way, his first name is Always!)

At times, we wrestle with a general feeling of unfulfillment, anxiety, or pure exhaustion. It's not connected to a specific event, but it's more like a cloud over our heads. Of course, these emotional states are symptoms of the harried lives we live. However, have you considered that we actually allow this to happen? I'm saying this with a spirit of love...and, to myself!

It's all about how we spend our limited and precious time. There are numerous demands for our attention, and many of them are worthy. Of course, we want to contribute to society, spend the weekends with our loved ones, and get that college degree. Yet, there are only so many hours in a day.

We can overcome this type of challenge by knowing our priorities, and learning how to protect ourselves from the time thieves. Every commitment should align with what's most important to us. Instead of doing more, only do what matters most.

Do you tend to feel over-committed? If so, that means you have a good heart because you want to help others. (It could also mean that you're avoiding something, but we'll address that in the chapters about fear and relationships.) Instead of automatically saying, "Yes!" to a request, tell the person you'll think about it. This way, you can verify that it fits your priorities. It also gives you time to think of another way to help, if possible. For example, maybe you can donate instead of volunteering at the fund raiser.

Are you anxious about the future? There is an entire chapter dedicated to this topic, so stay tuned! In the meantime, I encourage you to get the facts and resist the urge to paint a bleak picture of what's to come. As a good friend once told me, prepare for the worst, but hope for the best.

Having a firm foundation of knowing your priorities will sustain you when you get thrown a curveball. Everything in life can—and will—change. So, how do we face the inevitable dilemmas? Glad you asked!

CHARGING THROUGH CHALLENGES

1) What is the *exact* problem?

You feel depressed, but what's the cause? Oh, you got the invitation to your high school reunion. Why does this bother you? Is it because you don't feel accomplished enough? Maybe you've gained weight or lost your job.

If you keep asking why, eventually, the root cause will appear.

2) What are the obstacles? What do you fear?

It's unlikely that you'll lose those 50 pounds or get your MBA by next month. Perhaps you're afraid that your classmates will laugh at you or pity you.

3) What do you *want* to happen?

In other words, change the old habit of listing all the reasons why something will fail, and intentionally look at what can go right.

4) What are some possible solutions?

In this reunion example, you can sign up for a college course, and say, "I'm working on my MBA." You can probably lose ten pounds by the reunion, or get some shape wear, and ask a stylish friend for help with your outfit. Going to the event with someone is another way to boost your confidence. I always do that for my reunions!

5) Take action, darn it!

Although it's great to have a plan, it's more important to implement it. Don't get stuck in the paralysis of analysis. You don't even need to know the whole plan; just take the next step! It's better to try something and then redirect than it is to do nothing. Think of it this way: it's hard to steer a parked car.

6) Remember past victories

Surely, there have been times in your life when you succeeded at a task. That required certain attributes like resourcefulness or dedication. For instance, did you interview for your current or past job? That means you know how to make a good impression by dressing accordingly and showing confidence. Look! You already have what it takes to face that reunion!

If you possessed certain traits in the past, you could still use them in your current situation. As a note, you can always learn any needed skills, too.

7) Find encouragement

As social beings, we thrive when we're with people who understand and encourage us. Seek out like-minded souls. That may mean support groups, business owners' groups or a trusted friend.

Remember, you've survived 100% of the hardships you've faced so far. That's quite a track record, so keep going!

Life has four forces: love, suffer, struggle and win.

Whoever loves suffers. Whoever suffers struggles. Whoever struggles wins.

Love a lot, suffer a little, struggle bravely, and you always win.

—Oriana Fallaci

CHAPTER 2
NESSUN DORMA (NO ONE SLEEPS)

WHAT KEEPS YOU UP AT NIGHT?

In 1920, my grandfather arrived at Ellis Island with a small steamer trunk and big dreams. Most of his family remained in Italy while he and a few siblings crossed the ocean to pursue opportunities in America. Were they worried about life in the new world? Of course! Yet, they made the journey because their hopes for the future were bigger than their fears.

What keeps you up at night? If you're like most people, you worry about your loved ones' health and well-being, financial stability, and the condition of our world in general. A study conducted by Chapman University found that Americans' biggest fear these days is a corrupt government[1]. We'll address the Italian perspective on *that* in a future chapter of the book.

Gone are the days when public speaking was fear number one. People today are more afraid of sharks and oil spills than being on a podium. However, we can see from the study mentioned above that we'd rather be bitten by a snake or go to Hell than give a speech!

Fear and worry aren't the same. Fear can actually be helpful: we're wisely afraid of standing on the edge of a cliff with no railing. Worry, however, can cause physical and psychological damage if not kept in check.

It's been said that most of the things we worry about never even happen. That's a lot of wasted time and energy! Imagine how much happier and more peaceful our lives would be if we directed that focus on what we love instead of what causes anxiety.

Did you know that we humans are born with only two fears? Aside from the fear of falling and loud noises, everything else is learned. That's good news! If you're afraid of snakes, clowns or peanut butter sticking to the roof of your mouth (yes, it's a phobia!), you can unlearn it.[2] At the very least, it doesn't have to paralyze you.

My partner, Bob, is afraid of heights. That's usually not a problem unless we're working three stories above the sidewalk. When I first bought my grandparents' century-old house about seven years ago, we had to repair the outside of the porches. So, Bob hung onto the back of my jeans as I leaned over the railing to use a nail gun—which I'd never used before in my life—with my non-dominant hand. There were lots of creative combinations of expletives since I didn't do a very good job.

These days, Bob no longer breaks out in a sweat when we're on the third floor. Perhaps he got tired of my amateur work. (Heck, I'm a writer, not a carpenter!) Or, more likely, he overcame his fear of heights over time. Either way, he's proof that you can unlearn a fear.

Let's examine some of the more common fears that could be holding you back from experiencing your personal Renaissance. I'm sorry for not specifically addressing the aforementioned peanut butter fear! However, you'll see the pattern no matter what the phobia: you face it!

• Fear of the Future

Wouldn't it be great if we had a crystal ball that worked? We could prepare for the twists and turns of life…and see the winning lottery numbers!

Until time travel is invented, it's important to focus on what you *can* predict. For example, if you're worried about finances, commit to saving a little each month. Are you concerned about your family history of heart disease? Decide to eat well and exercise.

We're often afraid of our tomorrows because we think there's so much out of our control. Granted, we don't know if another company will buy ours and our jobs will be lost. Or, we worry about the future for our children, nieces and nephews. Whoever would've expected that something from another country would hold the world hostage? We live in uncertain times.

As mentioned before, prepare for the worst, but hope for the best. While there are many circumstances that we don't choose, we *do* have control over: preparing and hoping.

Without getting melodramatic, what's the worst that might happen? Figure out your Plan A, Plan B and, if you feel better, Plan C. Now that you're ready for any disaster, turn your attention to the way you'd like the situation to happen.

It's crucial to control your thoughts. Consciously overwrite the old and automatic script that's in your head. Instead of saying how scary your tomorrows may be, direct your inner dialogue to how life will be good or maybe even wonderful. You will feel less stressed and more optimistic. Your destiny awaits, and it will be a great adventure!

• Fear of Losing a Loved One

Part of worrying about the future is the heartbreaking thought of losing family and friends. Perhaps your son is deployed with the military, or your spouse is a firefighter. Your heart stops for a moment every time the phone rings. Past abandonment or death may be the cause of your fear.

While it's normal to dread any devastating event, it's important not to let your imagination run recklessly to the worst possible scenario. That constant state of stress will weaken your body and overwhelm your mind.

When this fear plagues us, we might try to push away people. We figure that it won't hurt as badly if they're only casual acquaintances. However, that leads to a shallow and lonely existence. Since you're reading this book, I know that's not what you want. You understand that life is more meaningful when we're connected to others.

Perhaps the pendulum swings to the other end: we cling so tightly to family and friends that they feel suffocated. We might even become manipulative, needy, or constantly demand attention. Holding onto love with a death grip is a sure way to kill it.

Most of us fall between the two extremes. We neither estrange nor strangle, but there will always be a tinge of anxiety that we may lose those we love. There is truth in that thought, and it accurately demonstrates the depth of our caring. It also reminds us of how precious those souls are to us.

No matter where you fall on the spectrum for this fear, the antidote is to change your thought patterns purposefully. Whenever you catch yourself getting pulled into the quicksand of panic, stop, breathe and give yourself a pep talk. Or call a trusted friend for some calming direction. Be proud that you care enough to worry about someone, but be wise enough to tone down any exaggerated thoughts.

Yes, things happen, and people may disappear from our lives. That's why we easily justify this fear of losing our loved ones. When it does happen, healing comes when we embrace the range of emotions and then take the time to grieve.

Whether it's the death of a relationship or an actual physical passing, remember that fear doesn't stop death; it stops life.

• Fear of Change

While there are no guarantees in life, there is an ironic constant: everything changes. Most people don't like change because it's uncomfortable and often unknown. Yet, it can also be a springboard to more joy, an opportunity to learn and to grow.

Often, we stay in a job we hate or a dysfunctional relationship because we think, *"What if there's nothing better?"* Sometimes, we don't make a choice. We get lose our job, or they walk out of our lives. Either way, the future doesn't seem promising—at first.

My father lived in the same Rhode Island neighborhood until he was almost 60 years old. His company was opening a facility in Tijuana, Mexico, and he was offered the job as the plant manager. For a guy who had no formal education, this was astounding. It was also—literally—across the country from everything he knew and loved. Further, at an age when many people start to scale down as they head toward retirement, he was possibly embarking on a new enterprise.

When my father asked my opinion of this dramatic move, I encouraged him to jump. If he didn't like it, he could always return home or perhaps go somewhere else. The bottom line was that he didn't want to have any regrets about not even trying. My father always told my siblings and me that we could do anything; it was time for him to heed his own words.

As you probably expect, given the tone of this book, he loved it! The house in Bonita, CA, had a fountain and lemon trees which reminded him of our families' homes in Italy. He enjoyed learning the ins and outs of running an international business, and he took pride in grooming his numerous employees to achieve their best.

Instead of being frozen with the fear of change, my father took the leap of faith. Would he have been happy if he hadn't moved? Probably. But, his outlook on life amped up because he took a chance and succeeded.

Another aspect of fearing change relates to our loved ones. In my father's case, the move meant living far away from his brother who—in my dad's words—was the wind beneath his wings. Perhaps you're concerned that your friends might not be too happy when you stop drinking, or your closest coworker might be jealous of your promotion. We may be excited about a different path, but our family and friends might not share our enthusiasm.

Once you've decided on that new direction, you can ease our loved ones' fear of change by reassuring them of their importance.

We can keep in touch so easily these days by phone calls and video chats. We can find other ways to spend time with our friends, and include them when appropriate.

Keep in mind that not everyone will stay in your life and that's okay. We still love them, wish them well, and keep the doors open. In some cases, it's for the best, anyway.

I challenge you to look at change as an opportunity. What do you *want* to happen? What can you do— today— to make it a reality? Even if you take only baby steps, those positive actions will conquer any discouraging thinking. Over time, you will achieve more than you can imagine.

- Fear of Failure

A few years ago, a couple took private language lessons with me before their trip to Italy. They brought along their seven-year-old daughter to each session. When I asked a review question in Italian, the daughter often responded before her parents. Why? One of the reasons is that young children don't have many negative associations with making mistakes like we adults do. She wasn't afraid to try.

We worry about being rejected and being judged. We may have painful memories of being laughed at or left out because of some errors we made. Some of these flashbacks are years or even decades old, and they still paralyze us today.

It's helpful to put our defeats in perspective: failure is not the opposite of success; it's a part of it. There are countless stories of famous people who didn't let failure deter them from achieving greatness. If one person did it, so can you. Failure isn't fatal if we learn from it.

A great resource for inspirational stories on this subject is Andy Andrews' series of books titled *Storms of Perfection*.[3] He shares stories from highly successful people of how they overcame trials and rejection, and ultimately reached the top of their fields.

I once heard that tragedy plus time equals humor. While this isn't always the case, it is another way to look at making mistakes.

Being able to laugh at our missteps can help us connect with others. I'll give you an example.

During my second trip to Italy, my language skills were elementary at best. I was at a big Sunday dinner at a friend's house; it was wonderful with everyone enjoying the food and fellowship. Someone asked me which cuisine was better, American or Italian.

To answer the question, I told them— with my limited linguistic skills— that I cook the same way as the Italians, but the ingredients in America seem to have more preservatives.

In general, you can pretty much add a vowel to the end of an English word and it will be close to the Italian counterpart. Well…that's not always true, as I embarrassingly discovered.

When I said, "…*piu' preservativi,*" conversations stopped and they all burst into laughter. You see, the Italian word for preservatives is "*conservanti*" and not the word I used. What I actually said was that the ingredients have more condoms. I can only imagine the pictures in their minds of American cooking!

I share that story with my Italian language students to help them relax. They see that they *will* make mistakes; it's part of the learning curve. As we find the humor in our hiccups, we connect because we relate to each other.

Blessed are those who can laugh at themselves, for they shall never cease to be amused.

No matter what life brings to your doorstep, I hope you face it with faith rather than fear. I encourage you to look at all your tomorrows confidently saying, "*Even* if…" rather than anxiously saying, "What if…?"

Taking action to combat worry gives you strength and a sense of control. With optimism and courage, you can break the bonds of fear.

Worry never robs tomorrow of its sorrow,
it only saps today of its joy.

—Leo Buscaglia

CHAPTER 3
INFERNO (HELL)

NOT DANTE'S, BUT MAYBE YOURS

I was sitting on an ocean view balcony in Maui. Sunlight danced on the water and the birds' songs floated on the soft breeze. Paradise, right? Not for me. Even in all that beauty and being with dear friends, my mind was shrouded with destructive thoughts.

I'd always felt like I was a mistake, and that anyone I loved would be better off without me. All the years of counseling kept me from doing anything drastic. I'd take even more time and discovery to say I'd finally overcome this enemy in my mind.

Am I now totally free from depression? I don't know that we're ever completely cured. I *do* know that my bouts on the dark side are now rare. Further, I can see them coming and prepare so that I'm not sucked into the black hole.

We all experience sadness; there's no escaping that. For some, though, an ominous cloud is always hovering and sometimes envelops us. Despite exhaustion, we can't sleep. Though we want joy in our lives, but it's too much effort to get out of our pajamas, let alone out of the house. We feel that Dante's sign at the entrance of hell —to abandon all hope— is addressed to us.

If you've battled depression or are in the midst of it right now, I have good news. You can slay that demon. I know this because I did.

Perhaps it's not you but someone you love who carries a heavy heart. This chapter will bring clarity to what they face and how to help. It'll also guide you on what you can— and can't —do to walk this path with them.

Please note that I don't claim to be an expert in this area. I hold no degrees in psychology. I'll simply share what helped me emerge from darkness into light.

The scene at the beginning of this chapter was during the lowest period of my life even though everything external (career, house, marriage) appeared to be perfect. More recently, I've faced the most difficult times in my life: devastating losses, divorce, being laid off twice, and financial woes. However, I didn't contemplate jumping off any balconies. What was the difference? I sought help and I learned techniques to survive and thrive despite of this life-long battle.

As you can guess from this book's theme, I attribute some of my progress to spending time in Italy and studying the culture. Am I suggesting that a trip to the *Bel Paese* will cure what ails you? Although it's worth a try (wink!), it's truly about incorporating the Italians' perspective and passion about life into my own. So, it's not only this chapter, but all of them that contribute to your *dolce vita* (sweet life).

You won't see many Italians or Italian-Americans openly discussing depression at the local café. That's because the *bella figura* (making a good impression) is crucial to everyday life. In fact, one study showed that 75% of Italians believe that the topic of depression should be avoided in public.[1] The study also reported that 90% of the respondents said that strong support from family and friends is necessary to overcome depression. So, we may not banter about this at a party, but we'll stand beside you arm in arm.

Depression is different from sadness, and it's wise to recognize the signs. Here are some symptoms of depression:

- Chronic feelings of despair and emptiness

- Loss of interest in favorite activities

- Insomnia or over-sleeping

- Trouble thinking, deciding, and concentrating

- Feelings of worthlessness or guilt

- Thoughts of suicide or how life would be better without you for those you love

If you or someone you care for exhibits those symptoms for weeks at a time or more, it could be depression. Getting help sooner instead of later will prevent this from becoming your identity and, ultimately, your destiny.

We can look at depression as a warning sign rather than a taboo condition. Just like increased ocean swells and a drop in barometric pressure are signals that a hurricane is likely, depression alerts us that an internal storm is brewing. By approaching this with a mix of logic and love, we can navigate into calmer seas. Further, we're addressing the cause of our depression rather than numbing it with alcohol, drugs or destructive behaviors.

WHEN SOMEONE YOU LOVE BATTLES DEPRESSION

Everyone responds to situations differently. We're not surprised when someone is heartbroken after a death or divorce; we all understand that. In contrast, one person may view his upbringing as dysfunctional, but his sibling remembers it as pleasant. Keep in mind that you may look at a situation as trivial, whereas your loved one is devastated. I'm not saying you're wrong; it's just that we can't judge how deeply a person is hurting.

When you first ask people how they're doing, they'll probably give you the automatic response of "fine." If you can tell that something is amiss, I suggest that you gently ask again. One of two things will happen. They'll snap at you or they'll open up to you. If it's the former, let it go for now. You could say something like, "Remember that you can always talk to me."

If the person does start to share, they want you *just to listen.* Unless they ask you what they should do or what you think, do *not* suggest solutions except if it's a matter of life and death. I know you only want to help and encourage your loved one, but they need to be heard before hearing any advice.

One of the worst things you can say is, "Don't feel bad." You then go on to tell of how you or other people have been through worse. It's like watching a one-upmanship contest. This doesn't make us suddenly realize that, *gee whiz, everything is actually okay.* The person is already telling himself that he shouldn't feel like this, and he's frustrated and maybe ashamed that he can't just snap out of it.

Beyond that, simply being there and staying in touch goes further than you might think. A quick text message or phone call can lift someone's spirits because they realize that they aren't alone. Just knowing that I can call a close friend gives me strength. I don't even have to pick up the phone; the simple belief that they're there makes me walk a little taller.

When offering help, don't say something vague like, "Let me know what I can do." At times, that person may not even know what he wants or needs. So, it's more productive to offer something specific like picking up some dinner to share or offering to mow their lawn.

You may feel helpless, and maybe even afraid to see this treasured person wrestle with depression. You want to fix it. With your love and with time, there are sunnier days ahead.

Having said all that, I implore you to get professional and immediate help if you see signs of suicide or other destructive behaviors. Some situations are beyond what a layman can handle.

WHEN DEPRESSION IS YOUR BATTLE

Whenever I meet someone who has experience with this siege on our minds, I instantly relax. I don't need to explain much or justify it at all. We're comrades.

Dear reader, know that my words here are to bring encouragement and to give you hope. You won't find judgment but, instead, tactics that helped me. I share this with empathy and, sometimes, a little tough love.

Some of you have faced horrific events that have opened the door to depression. I can't imagine the anguish of someone who has experienced the loss of a child, rape, war, or any of the myriad of heartaches this world can bring. While my suggestions in this chapter may seem shallow compared to what you need, I hope that you'll at least find a spark of belief in a brighter future. Take as much time as you need to heal.

No matter what has caused your depression, getting professional help may be the best route for you. Further, there is no shame in meeting with a counselor. Sometimes, a person looking into your life from the outside can offer a refreshing perspective.

It's wise to know your symptoms and triggers so that you can be proactive. For me, insomnia and constant doubts are a few signs of a downward spiral. To give you an analogy, it feels like I'm floating on a river, and I'm approaching a waterfall. The plunge may seem inevitable, but I remind myself that it's not.

When I see that waterfall on the horizon, I'm vigilant about the people I spend time with when possible. That's a short list of names, by the way. I try to surround myself with those who understand and encourage me. Face to face is best, but you don't *have* to put on pants or leave the house. You can pick up the phone, write an email, or log onto a video chat. Just don't stand up during that last one if you're in your undies!

Sometimes, it's necessary to put on a happy face while at work or at an important event. Yes, it can be exhausting, but I want to honor my commitments and behave accordingly. You see, it's not always about us. There are times when I don't have the luxury to act the way I feel, but I have the responsibility to act the way I should. Not only is that just being an adult, but it's also the *bella figura* attitude that we'll explore in chapter nine.

It's important to take care of yourself when you're in the middle of the black cloud of depression. Following are six steps to self care.

➤ Soothe

What helps you to relax? For some, that means listening to music or taking a walk, For others, maybe relaxation involves a massage or yoga. Make a list of calming activities; have some that you can do anywhere and others that require more time or changing locations.

➤ Spark

It's equally important to identify what energizes you. Playing with your pets, listening to your favorite comedian, or dancing in your living room (curtains closed, of course!) are ways to lift your spirits. Some of you go for a run. As a note, if you ever see me running, you should run, too; it means something scary is chasing me!

➤ Sun

Some days, we want to stay home and eat ice cream. We should at least take a shower and get dressed. You get *cannoli* points (instead of brownie points!) if you go outside or at least sit by a window. The sun's vitamin D may lift your spirits and boost brain activity. This is vital if you also suffer from seasonal affective disorder.

➤ Sit up

No matter where you are—in the living room or the boardroom— remember to have good posture and breathe deeply. When we're blue, we tend to slouch which can lead to shallow breathing. I'm sure you agree that we need to have more oxygen going to our brains rather than less.

➢ Skip

Knowing what *not* to do is also important to your sanity. I strongly suggest avoiding the nightly news, horror movies, and even social media. The latter may surprise you. We end up comparing our seemingly boring and sad existence to the highlights of others' magnificent and glamorous lives. Trust me, those smiling faces in front of the Tower of Pisa were fighting earlier in the day over who forgot the phone chargers.

➢ Square Meals

Depending on my level of depression, my eating habits vary. If I'm at rock bottom, I tend to skip meals. If I'm only sad, I might consume mass quantities of carbs. Neither of those dietary plans is healthy. It's best to have regular meals and snacks low in sugar and refined carbohydrates. Many people's moods improve when they include foods (or supplements) rich in Omega-3 fatty acids and B vitamins. Check with your doctor first, of course!

———✺———

Now for the tough love that I realize applies to a small number of readers, but needs to be addressed. Is it possible that you are *choosing* to stay in a state of depression? Why would anyone do that? Change can be terrifying. Even though the crushing sadness is dreadful, it's familiar. It's like someone who stays in a bad relationship: the fear of something new is greater than the pain he or she feels.

Another reason a person decides to stay downtrodden is that they like the attention. Ouch! I experienced this firsthand the week before writing this chapter. Once again, life threw me a nasty curveball, and I started to head toward the waterfall. My

THE ITALIAN ART OF LIVING

partner, Bob, recognized this and went out of his way to treat me with extra TLC.

Since my primary love language is physical touch, I was lovin' his language![2] I thought, *"Hmmm...I'm getting more hugs and sweet words than usual. Maybe I should stay sad all the time."* Don't worry; I finally came to my senses!

If you've done this, please examine how this behavior affects relationships. I feel that it borders on manipulation because we're taking advantage of someone else's kindness. They'll eventually feel used and grow tired of the drama. Is that what we want? No. Meaningful relationships are built on trust and respect instead of playing head games.

———

Through this dark journey, we may feel broken and worthless. I'd like you to think about the beautiful mosaics that adorn so many churches like St. Mark's Basilica in Venice. They were created with thousands of tiny pieces—*broken* pieces—and yet, they are works of art. So, my dear, are you.

Remember, too, that when you overcome this struggle, you can then help someone else. You can tell them that, even in our darkest days, hope is real and you're the proof.

This isn't about instantly going from despair to joy. That's unrealistic. It's about taking one step today and taking another step tomorrow. Use the principles in this chapter to remind you to do something, anything, to feel better.

Depression drains our energy and happiness, but it doesn't have to rule our lives. With some incremental actions and a little faith, you'll eventually climb out of the cavern of despair and stand on the mountaintop where you can see a bright future.

Finchè c'è vita, c'è speranza.

(As long as there is life, there is hope.)

—Italian proverb

CHAPTER 4
BASTA! (ENOUGH!)

BREAK THE CYCLE

Uncle Johnny (my father's brother) was a quiet, pensive, and devoted man. He was my godfather and my "second dad". While he was always a key part of my life, we became inseparable after our trip to Italy in 2001. When I lived out of state, we spent every Sunday night on the phone for an hour or more.

A close relative had wrongly accused him of doing something hurtful and disloyal. Although Uncle Johnny and other family members tried to set things right, this relative held onto the grudge.

Since this person's spouse passed away years before, the date of death for the unforgiving relative was blank on the tombstone. Uncle Johnny continually asked the children to have the date engraved, but *someday* became never.

During one of my trips to the cemetery, I visited "Mattera Row" and noticed the date of death had been added to the stone. You guessed it: Uncle Johnny had it done. Even though he had every right to wash his hands of that person, he did what was proper and honorable.

Forgiveness doesn't mean that the other person was right. Instead, it shows the goodness of your heart. Mature and honest people recognize that no one is perfect; we all stumble.

Remember, too, being unforgiving hurts you more than the evildoer, especially if he or she doesn't care. It's like you drinking poison, hoping that the other person dies. It only eats away at *your* peace and health.

Here's another way to think of this: you're letting the offender win twice, first when they hurt you, and then every time you mentally replay the scene. Is that what you really want? I doubt it.

All of us has felt the devastating sting of betrayal, heartbreak, and loss caused by another. People have done the unthinkable to us or those we love. We plan our revenge; sure that justice will be served to the transgressor on a cold platter.

Several years ago, one such offense occurred that ripped apart my family and was specifically directed at me. I won't bore you with the details. Just know that it was all about money.

By the way, many people misquote the Bible about money being the root of all evil. No, the *love* of money is the source of wickedness. Money is only a tool. Have you ever seen a dollar bill slap someone or a nickel rob a store? No. Good people will do good deeds with money; you know what bad people do.

But I digress…

There were two kingpins in the plot that divided my family. I was shocked that blood relatives could do this to one another. My hatred for the injustice, lies, and greed took a toll on my physical and emotional health.

I spent nights awake, replaying the scenarios, and thinking about how I could exact sweet revenge. I toyed with the idea of reporting them to the authorities or at least sending anonymous letters threatening them with exposure. (Sinister laughter goes here!) Oh, to watch karma visit them would be marvelous, wouldn't it?

Last year, I ran into someone who knows the whole ugly story. He asked if I'd heard about kingpin number two having brain cancer. The saying is that karma is a female dog, and here she finally bit someone. Did I feel vindicated?

If you've watched Italian-American mobster movies or TV series, you probably have an answer. You could imagine that I was overjoyed that someone who—in your best *Godfather* voice—disrespected us and got what they deserved. Yes, there's a thread of that in my culture—in any culture.

Upon hearing the news about the cancer, I felt nothing. *Nothing.* How odd since I thought I'd be doing the *Mambo Italiano.* Yet, it occurred to me that a person's penalty for their sins doesn't change what they did or make up for it. If I gloat in my enemies' misfortunes, am I any better than them? Further, since I had no part in that person's adversity, I have no possible guilt.

Vengeance isnt going to make the world a better place; it's only going to perpetuate the hurt and the hate. We may feel like tough guys to say that we don't get mad; we get even. But when will it end? By choosing to break that cycle, we become better rather than bitter, and the future is now hopeful.

Please don't misunderstand me: I believe that evil must be judged. Thieves, murderers, and child abusers should atone for their crimes through the proper channels. No, the system doesn't always work, and innocent souls are sometimes victims. But before we take matters into our hands, we need to ask if it's truly our place. Think about it—investigators are often not allowed to work on a case if they're too close to the situation.

Keep in mind that the relationship may never return to how it was before the infraction. You'll never speak to some people again because they're not willing to change. Yes, it's sad, but that's their choice. Instead, *you* will break loose from the shackles that tied you to the pain. By choosing forgiveness, you can learn from the experience and release yourself freely to the future. We can hope that they, too, will come to this same decision someday.

One more note about this topic—you may feel that I've minimized some horrific traumas such as abuse or terrorism. That's certainly not my intention, and I don't claim to be an expert. You may need guidance from a qualified professional such as a therapist or a pastor. There's no shame in needing help. It won't be easy, but you can overcome it; others have, and so can you.

I'd be remiss if I left out two more areas of forgiveness. When we caused someone else's pain, we may think they deserved it or that no one can truly understand what they did. Remember, this isn't just about the other person; it's about peace in *your* heart and moving forward.

If you say to that person you hurt, "I'm sorry, *but...*" you aren't sincere. You may need more time to admit to your role in the situation. Am I suggesting that you wait? No.

Almost two years after my father passed away, my mother misunderstood something I said, but I wasn't aware. For a year, she was cordial but distant. Whenever I asked, she said everything was fine.

After many months of this behavior, my mother finally told me why. At first, I was angry because we'd wasted a year. My father's death at 70 years old was—and is—a constant reminder of life's brevity. Of course, I was sorry I'd hurt my mother, *but* it wasn't intentional. It wasn't *my* fault, was it?

I relayed the tale to Uncle Johnny. After all, he was my god-father and, therefore, spiritual guide. His response to me was, "She's your mother." That's all he needed to say. He was referring to the 5th Commandment which is about honoring your parents. It doesn't say to honor them *if* they act a certain way or do par-ticular things. Nope. It says to honor them. Period.

After having a little pity party, I called my mother and apol-ogized. I left out the *but* because that was my issue to wrestle and not hers. I'd offended my mother, and asking for a pardon was the right thing to do.

Was this the worst way that I've ever hurt someone? Absolutely not! I'm human and have committed my share of unkind acts. This story is to bring home the point of taking action now. You see, my mother passed away not too long after that. If I'd waited another year, I would've been begging for absolution at a grave site.

Don't wait another day to try and make things right. Ask the person you hurt how you can atone for your actions, and then do it. No matter what, focus on rebuilding trust. Maybe you have to pour liquor down the drain. If it's financial, get a second job to replenish the squandered bank accounts. By showing that person that you're serious about making up for your mistakes, you'll likely salvage the relationship.

For Heaven's sake, don't continue to put yourself in the situation to let it happen again! Quit going to the casino or the local bar. Stop frequenting that coffee shop where you flirt with the attractive barista. If you're wrestling with an addiction, there are support groups that have successfully helped others in your shoes.

Reel in your pride, remember that you're not perfect, and seek reconciliation. Even if the person doesn't accept your apology, you've done what you could and should.

What about that third area of forgiveness? You may need to forgive yourself.

Perhaps you're mad at yourself for missed opportunities, staying in a bad relationship, or being taken advantage of—again. Maybe you've made some bad life choices like cheating on your spouse or gambling away your child's college fund. It could be that the last words you said to someone were hateful, and now that person is gone. You might think you don't deserve to be pardoned.

The first technique to try is changing your perspective. What if your best friend did the shameful deed? What would you say? More than likely, you'd agree with your friend that it was a dreadful mistake, and there may be consequences. You'd say that we can't change the past, but we can do something now.

You would probably *not* tell your friend that he's the biggest jerk ever to have lived. You wouldn't say there's no hope or that he might as well just give up on life. So, why do we say those things to ourselves? Those thoughts don't help; they only hurt us *and* the people we love.

Not forgiving ourselves—and the shame that goes along with it—is a prison. We don't only think that we did something wrong; we think that *we* are what's wrong. We must remember that we chose to make those mistakes. Did you catch that? We *chose* to do it. That doesn't make us evil; it makes us human. Further, that means we can now choose to do what's right.

What if the person you wronged has passed away or your children won't speak to you? There are still ways to move forward like volunteering for a cause near and dear to that person's heart. You might become a Big Brother or Big Sister. There are abundant opportunities to prove to yourself and others that you're worthy of forgiveness.

If you don't forgive, you don't fully live. Forgiveness doesn't change the past, but it does bring hope to the future. Holding on to the hurt ties you to suffering. Learn from the lesson, and you'll grow. Decide to be better than what broke you so that you live your life from a place of power instead of pain.

It is in pardoning that we are pardoned.

—Francis of Assisi

CHAPTER 5
WHEN IN ROME...

HABITS & THE SONS OF TOMMY TREES

I n Italian, the "when in Rome" saying translates to "countries that you travel (to), customs you will find." The word for "custom" is *usanza* which also means "habit". They're closely related concepts in English, too.

Habits are the brain's way to conserve energy. Can you imagine if we had to remind ourselves to blink or breathe? Think of habits as programmed shortcuts in your mind's GPS to get you through life. It takes a lot less concentration to drive to your favorite restaurant than to figure out where that new one is located.

Learning new behaviors can be challenging especially if we're particularly fond of the old ones (eating comes to mind). Therefore, it's critical to focus on *why* you're making these changes. You may even plan rewards for achieving certain milestones. Perhaps you think that's childish, but it could be the spark that you need to keep going.

Even when we've reached that pinnacle of success, we can fall back into those old habits in the blink of an eye. Why is that? I call it the sons of Tommy trees. Let me explain.

My next-door neighbors in Colorado lived in the oldest house in the development. So, Tommy and his family also had the tallest trees on the block. One day, his mini forest was gone! He had them all cut down because they were interfering with his satellite reception. (Gasp!)

The next summer, little trees sprouted all over my yard. Through the years, the root system of Tommy's trees had spread, yet none of us saw them in our lawns before then. It was because of the right circumstances that happened at the right time. Bloop, bloop, bloop, bloop, bloop...little sons of Tommy trees everywhere.

That happens with our habits, too. We may lose weight, quit smoking or stop gambling, and then—out of the blue—we eat an entire pizza and light up a cigarette while calling our bookie. That's because the right circumstances happened at the right time.

Our habits are like the root system of Tommy's trees. Even though our figurative forest is now a field, particular situations plus timing can cause that old nature to sprout. Bloop, bloop, bloop, bloop, bloop! That explains why it seems so easy to fall back into old patterns.

This isn't to discourage you, but it's to forewarn you. It happens to the best of us. When it does, we can return to what helped us develop a good habit in the first place.

Certainly, this chapter addresses how to improve our physical routines like diet and exercise. Let's not forget that our mental habits or thought patterns can also sabotage us.

Using the analogy of the brain as a computer, the programs in your mind were written months and even years ago. They're intimately tied to events and emotions from your history. So, when we get up in the morning, we're already living in the past! Don't lose heart, though, because you can write new programs today so that, five years from now, your mind will awaken encouraged and empowered.

Think of it this way: every day, we're playing that same ol' song on an 8-track or maybe on a Victrola. This can be good when it comes to our core values and traditions we want to keep intact. It's often something that sabotages our health and happiness.

Further, defeating self-talk isn't usually true, but we keep hearing the message on repeat.

I'll give you an example. I was chubby as an adolescent and teenager. Sometimes, children aren't very tactful about what they say to others. They called me names like "tree stump" because I couldn't run very quickly. A teenager even said he didn't want to date me because of my weight.

Fast forward to my late 30s and I was slender and stylish. As I walked to a business meeting, I approached a playground filled with children and I froze. That old recording of youngsters taunting me played in my head. Can you guess what those little rascals did when I passed by the playground? Yep. Nothing! My obsolete and false programming caused me to panic needlessly.

It takes a conscious effort to update the software in our systems. Don't worry if your computer still runs on punch cards or floppy disks because it's never too late to become the best version of yourself. Just zip up your Members Only jacket and get started today!

Did you know an IT specialist is working in your brain right now? It's your Reticular Activating System (RAS). This protects your mind from getting overloaded and helps you to focus. You've already met RAS. Let's say your favorite cousin Tony gets a new black Cadillac. All of a sudden, you see black Caddys everywhere. That's your RAS working.

You can harness the power of your RAS to create habits that lead to achieving your goals. Let's say one way you want to be healthier is to eat dinners at home. At this point, *how* you'll do it is secondary; that comes later. By deciding *what* you want, your RAS goes into action and activates your search engine. Like Tony's Cadillac, you'll start to find quick and low-calorie ideas all around you via a magazine at the check-out lane or a coworker raving about a dish she prepared last night.

As you pay attention to the suggestions, you'll discover more and more. It's similar to when you do an internet search for boots; banner ads for footwear pop up in almost every website you visit after that. Your RAS radar will now alert you to countless options to get what you want.

YOUR BLUEPRINT FOR BETTER BEHAVIORS

1) Identify *one* habit you want to change.

- What are the long-term consequences if you don't change it? For example, if you keep spending $5 each weekday for a fancy coffee, that's $1,250 a year or $58,000 throughout a career. Wow. That puts it in perspective!

2) What positive action will you do instead?

- Most of us can't just stop doing something; we have to replace it with a new behavior. That's because our minds don't work in the negative. To prove that, I want you to *not* think about a pineapple pizza. You're not thinking about a pineapple pizza, are you? Of course you are! That's because to not think about it, you have to think about it. That's why kids in those funny videos always run into the tree or mailbox. They're thinking, "I don't want to hit that tree!" The brain doesn't register the "don't"; it only focuses on the tree. And please never eat pineapple on your pizza!

3) What are the benefits of the new behavior? What's the best possible outcome?

- Obviously, anything health-related will lead to a longer and higher-quality life. Time-related habits, like being with family and friends instead of being glued to a screen, will add joy. Only using cash instead of racking up the credit cards will lead to financial stability.

4) Take action!

- What are three possible ways to implement the new behavior? Do at least one of them each day.

- When possible, add the new practice to a habit you already have. For example, listen to a motivational podcast while drinking your usual cup of coffee.

- Tell a good friend or two about your plan. Accountability is a great motivator to stay on track.

5) Repeat, repeat, repeat the behavior.

- No matter how many days the gurus say it takes to create a new habit, they all agree that it's a matter of repetition. No, it's not sexy, but it's effective.

Once you follow the blueprint for one habit, simply apply it to the next area of your life where you want to improve. Like snowflakes, they'll add up to a blizzard of success.

Italians intuitively use habits to live longer and to have more meaningful lives. In fact, Italy boasts one of the world's Blue Zones (areas that are home to an unusually high number of residents 100 years old or more). The phenomenon is so extraordinary that it's captured the attention of the global scientific community and has sparked Blue Zone Cities in other countries.

Of course, the Mediterranean diet is one key. Perhaps you can get in the routine of eating more fresh vegetables and less processed foods. I'm not saying we can't have *cannoli* or chicken parmesan, just not all the time. One *gelato* won't clog my arteries, but having one every day compounds caloric interest right on my thighs.

Another Blue Zone indicator is being active. Sardinia, Italy, has the world's highest number of males over 100, and it's attributed to walking. Shepherds there cover five or more miles a day while tending their flocks. You don't have to buy a sheep, but you could walk while on the phone or do some push-ups during TV commercials.

We all know that Italy was dealt a crippling blow in 2020. You'd think that Sardinia would have the highest number of fatalities since it has the oldest population. However, they had one of the lowest death rates: less than a *tenth* of a percent! That's especially remarkable since 13,000 northern Italians escaped to their vacation homes on Sardinia. There's something to be said about their way of life that keeps them strong!

Those who studied the Italian centenarians also noticed the close-knit communities in the Blue Zones. In Italy, the elderly are lovingly cared for and respected. Gianni Pes, the Italian researcher who first coined the Blue Zone phrase, said, "The generous affection and care they get from loved ones has been shown to protect against age-related diseases and slow cognitive degeneration. People who live alone beyond the age of 80 have a much shorter life expectancy than those who have close family ties."

I know some of you just groaned at this and said, "But, you don't know my family!" We'll discuss relationships more in future chapters. I encourage you to reach out to someone you love with a quick call or message. Set a reminder to do that once a week. It's not just family ties that enrich our lives but the bonds of friendship, too. No, you don't have to call your drama queen aunt—at least not today.

We become experts at whatever we practice, good or bad. If you play the piano every evening, you'll perform concerts one day. If we spend many of our waking hours hearing about floods, famines, violence, and disease, we'll end up stressed and depressed. Let's get out of the habit of willingly putting horrible images into our minds. Instead, let's focus on what we want in our lives. Our thinking—positive or negative—affects our emotions, which guides our actions and, ultimately, become our reality. Isn't it better, then, to have more encouraging thoughts going into our minds?

Similarly, many people are almost addicted to talking about their problems. You might not be a guest on one of those crazy he-said-she-said TV shows, but are you constantly bringing up your woes to anyone who'll listen? Yes, it's important to be open and real, but there's a time and place for discussing your dilemmas. Don't be that person who always complains. Instead, be that person who talks about joy, love, hope, and success.

I also encourage you to start working on new behaviors now. Don't wait for some life event to scare you into doing it. We can learn new habits when we're relaxed and simply want to improve, or we can wait until we're shocked and forced into making changes. Which do you think is better?

Further, let's start creating the habits today that'll be the foundation for our future selves. Picture how you want your life to be in ten years. What are you doing each day? How is your health? How do you treat others?

Today, start acting as if you're already there. I don't mean to buy that fancy sports car this weekend! Yet, you can make choices right now that fit the image of your ideal life. Developing those habits now will only help you achieve those goals. It doesn't cost anything to make better choices. Let's implement those life-improving habits today!

All new behaviors take time, and small steps will accumulate, so keep going. If you smoke one less cigarette today, you can eventually get to zero. If you listen to one inspiring podcast, that's time you didn't spend reliving past hurts. Celebrate the small wins because they'll add up to a life of *abbondanza* (abundance)!

Good habits are the key to all success. Bad
habits are the unlocked door to failure.

—Og Mandino

CHAPTER 6
PAESAN'! (MY FELLOW AMERICAN, UM, ITALIAN!)

BELL TOWERS & THE ART OF FRIENDSHIP

Would you be interested in something that helps you live longer, stay mentally sharp, handle stress better, and boosts happiness? If so, this chapter is for you. Common sense and numerous scientific studies recognize the abundant benefits of friendship. There's also a correlation between loneliness and a multitude of health problems including high blood pressure and reduced immunity.

Dante Alighieri, author of *The Divine Comedy*, said that we can't have a perfect life without friends. I believe that wholeheartedly. True friends are sometimes more of a family to us than our blood relatives. We *choose* to stand by each other with a sense of love and loyalty rather than a possibly forced sense of duty.

A cousin in Italy once said to me, "A friend is a friend. It's all or nothing." Although I don't remember my parents ever saying those words, we were raised with that mindset. Friends are an extension of the family, which means there are more to face the difficulties of life together.

The Italians' perspective of friendship has been cultivated through the centuries and around the bell towers. Let me explain.

Imagine you're traveling internationally and meet a pleasant family at a café. You ask where they're from, and they reply, "Oh, we're Americans." Later in the conversation, you discover that they're from Providence, Rhode Island.

If you struck up that same conversation with a family from the boot-shaped peninsula, they'd likely say that they were Florentines rather than first describe themselves as Italians.

Americans self-identify in the order of country/state/city, but Italians do the opposite: city/"state"/country. Why is that? There are two main reasons: one is about simple geography and the other is about who can be trusted.

With mountain ranges, islands, plains, and volcanoes, traveling through Italy can be a challenge even in our modern era. Before airplanes and high-speed trains, going from one region to another was particularly daunting. Each area became self-sufficient out of necessity and fiercely proud of what they accomplished together. They had their traditions and dialects. This geographical separation also sparked a sense of doubt and suspicion of people from other towns. Hold this thought as we look at reason number two.

When non-Europeans think about Italy, most believe it's been a country since the Roman Empire. That's not true, however. Unified Italy, as we know it today, has existed since 1861, and has been a republic only since 1946.

Throughout the centuries, it's been invaded and ruled by a myriad of countries and leaders. Whether it was the Greeks or the Huns, emperors or dictators, the Italian people learned the only ones you can really trust are your family and friends. Your community is the next ring in a circle of confidence. Anyone outside that perimeter is questionable.

This is where the term *campanalismo* comes into play. There is no direct English translation, but it speaks to the pride and love one has for his or her birthplace. It's derived from the Italian word for bell tower (*campanile*), which is usually the highest, most visible structure in the town. Michelangelo said he never wanted to live where he couldn't see the *Duomo*. (Okay, so that's the cathedral rather than the bell tower, but you get the point!)

The bell tower was the symbol of all the good in that city: traditions, food, achievements, and family and friends. Think about how you feel when you see a picture of the Statue of Liberty, a soaring eagle, or watch your team win a championship. If those ignite your patriotism, you've just experienced *campanalismo*!

KEEPING THE BELL TOWER STRONG

Having dear and trusted friends doesn't just happen. I'm not saying that it's difficult, but it does take an effort to keep any relationship alive. With our fast-paced lives, we're pulled in different directions and constantly face crises that often leave us drained. At the end of the day, we just want to go to sleep. We tell ourselves, *"I'll call (name) tomorrow."* That becomes a week and then a month which compounds when your friends are in different time zones.

What if it's been ages since you contacted a particular person? You may feel awkward because of the delay. She probably feels the same way. If she called you, wouldn't you be happy? So, pick up that phone or send a quick text message.

Hey, what are you doing still reading this? Put down the book and call your friend right now! I'll wait for you. (The theme from *Jeopardy!* goes here.)

There! Don't you feel better now?

The focus here is about *being* a friend rather than *having* friends; a subtle but important difference. Don't sit around waiting for others. Heed the words of my great aunt Filomena: "Don't call your friends only when you need them." Make an effort and you'll reap the benefits of a happier, healthier, and longer life.

- Contact at least one friend each week. Set a reminder in your calendar.

- Plan "phone dates" for long-distance friends.

- When physically possible, plan to meet in person. Schedule the next get-together before you leave.

- Random acts of kindness: if you see a funny card or their favorite candy, send it to them.

One more note about keeping friendships strong is to remember to tell your friends *why* they're important to you. Appreciation reminds you of how blessed you truly are and fills your friend's heart as well. I'm not talking about loving someone with conditions. Instead, I'm encouraging you to verbalize what you treasure in that person and what makes him unique.

You can say things like, "Your positive attitude inspires me," or "I'm grateful that you listen without judgment," or "Knowing that you've got my back keeps me going!"

Since we're constantly bombarded with negative input, an inspiring message will be a ray of sunshine. Your words of valuing that person will lift her up—and fortify your bell tower.

Do you see that appreciation can work in every relationship? Whether it's your family or coworkers, start telling people the goodness you recognize in them. As long as you are sincere, you'll be amazed at how they respond.

ADDING TO YOUR BELL TOWER

One of the best ways to make new friends is by getting out of the house to do things you already enjoy. Walking your four-legged family member will help you to meet other dog lovers. Going to a dance class, joining a bocce club, or volunteering will put you in the company of like-minded people.

Another useful resource to expand your circle is Meetup.com which has groups of all types in all parts of the world. You can connect with hikers, photographers, entrepreneurs, cooks and artists. (Yes, there are some wild and crazy groups, too!) In every place I've lived, I've joined the Italian Meetup.com groups. I'm still in touch with many of the *paesani* from those cities even though I've since moved back to New England.

You may be saying, "But Dawn, what do I say to these people?" Here are some tips:

- Ask open-ended questions following the FRIEND acrostic. Of course, you don't have to use every one of these!

  Family (Children? Siblings?)
  Recreation (How do they spend their free time?)
  Interesting places they've been (Why did they go there? What did they like most?)
  Everyday details (Where do they work? Can they recommend a dentist or a tailor?)
  Nice sweater (or tie or shoes)! (People love compliments. Say why you like it.)
  Delicious restaurants in the area? (You can be specific: pizza, breakfast, or café.)

- Use their name a few times. Not only will it help you to remember it, but it shows you're truly interested.

- Remember details so you can ask your new friend about them the next time you meet.

- Focus on the person speaking rather than looking at everyone coming and going around you. It's as if you're only with him or her until a better prospect arrives.

- Truly listen to what they are saying versus thinking about what you're going to say next.

An interesting difference (to me, anyway) between Americans and Italians is what's considered taboo to discuss with people you don't know well. In the United States, it's impolite to talk about politics or religion, especially at the dinner table. Italians, on the other hand, are ready to debate just about any topic.

During my first visit to Italy, I was sitting between my dad and Uncle Johnny at a big family dinner. Two of our cousins sitting at opposite ends of the long table had differing opinions about a local politician. Voices escalated and they were soon standing and yelling at each other with hands gesturing like exclamation points to their arguments.

My dad leaned over to me and asked, "What would your mother do if she were here right now?" Since she was a seventh-generation southern belle, we agreed that she'd slide under the table to avoid the conflict.

However, my Italian relatives around that table never even flinched. The two red-faced cousins soon sat down, and everything was back to a pleasant Sunday dinner with no hard feelings and no evil eyes.

I bring this up because I feel that our society is offended too quickly these days. We put up barriers without finding out why someone holds certain beliefs. Granted, some people are plain rude, but why should we let a person like that ruin our day? Further, there are some people we'll never be best buddies with because of different core values. Yet, we can still be civilized and respectful even if they aren't.

We can't control what other people do or say. We can, however, take responsibility for how we react. In other words, don't get your *mutande* (undies) in a bunch! You'll make and keep more friends that way!

If you're having difficulty interacting with others, you might want to check your RBF (resting b*tch face). You know that facial expression you see when you catch yourself in a mirror? That's your RBF, and some of us look scary!

My relaxed expression makes others think I'm sad or annoyed. This is rarely the case, but they don't want to risk finding out if it's true. Further, at my age, the facial furrows are permanent. So, when I smile, the wrinkles hide in a pleasant face instead of a grumpy one.

REMODELING THE BELL TOWER

As people change and grow, relationships are tested. Many times, our friends grow with us or they accept the changes and still treasure what we have. Sadly, some of our friendships can turn toxic and leave us feeling let-down rather than loved.

This can happen especially when you make a lifestyle change like losing weight or giving up alcohol. If the relationship is based on hot fudge sundaes or getting buzzed, it may not survive when we try to improve our health. This may sound harsh, but if your friends don't support you, are they really your friends?

I'm not saying that we must agree 100% with everything. I have dear friends with different political and spiritual views, so we concentrate on what we have in common. We find other ways that we can spend time together.

There are some signs that your friends may not be open to a new and improved you. If you see some of these often, it's time for a heart-to-heart talk. Or it might be time to say, "*addio!*"

• Putting you down or embarrassing you

Good-natured teasing is one thing, but hurtful comments are unacceptable, especially in public. We trust our friends to tell us something that we may want to change in private. If someone keeps shaming you or making you feel like you're somehow less than they are, that's not a healthy relationship.

• Isolating you

Toxic people will try to keep you all to themselves; they want to be the constant center of your attention. They can be expert manipulators; one day, you'll realize that your family and other friends have drifted out of your life.

• Emotionally blackmailing you

Let's say you accepted an invitation to a members-only event. A true friend will tell you to have a great time, let you borrow that fabulous coat, and ask for details later. A toxic friend may pout or give you the cold shoulder because he thinks you shouldn't go without him.

• Draining you

Healthy friendships are give and take. When you get together, it's not over-the-top warm and fuzzy every time. However, if you always feel stressed or depleted after being with a person, that's a warning sign that you're in a destructive duo.

As awkward as it may be, the open and mature thing to do with toxic friends is to talk with them. Yes, it's easier to let them drift away over time. However, if it's someone you value, I encourage you to share your heart.

You may discover an explanation for their behavior, and perhaps you can help them. We never know what's happening in someone's life. They'll either be relieved that you care enough to save the friendship or they'll storm off in a huff. If it's the latter, let them go. You can sleep at night knowing that you tried.

FRAMILIES (FRIENDS THAT ARE LIKE FAMILY)

Looking at the Ellis Island ship manifest, Francesco Corsi (my partner's great grandfather) and Dante Simone are listed one after the other. They were both from the same small town and had big dreams. Francesco and Dante understood the importance of friendship, especially when facing a daunting challenge. The descendants of Francesco and Dante—both in America and in Italy—are friends even today.

If you have lived the friendship-making principles shared in this chapter, there are probably people in your life who've stood beside you, supported you and loved you, in good times and bad.

They are the ones you could call, any time of the day or night, and they'd answer. You trust and respect each other without question. Those are the friends who are more like family.

When I lived in Colorado, my community had numerous military families. That meant mothers and fathers who were deployed for months at a time, and many of us had no blood relatives in driving distance. The names on the mailboxes represented a wide range of ethnicities and faiths.

You may think that's sad, and it could've been. However, we pulled together and became brothers and sisters. We "adopted" their children who still call me "Aunt Dawn" 20+ years later. We spent holidays together, helped paint houses, and maintained cars. We celebrated birthdays and weddings, and we shed tears for tragedies that pierced our circle.

Perhaps you're like me: my parents are gone along with the days of big family gatherings. My closest sibling lives over a thousand miles from me. It's easy to feel like an orphan. Or, your nearby relatives are the fractured family members discussed in the next chapter.

My point is that sometimes we have to *make* our own families. It's not about quantity; it's about a select few friends who help, trust, respect, love, and honor each other, no matter what.

Think of it this way: would you rather have a hundred diamond chips or three stunning solitaires? Be dedicated to nurturing those rare and precious relationships. Treat them like the treasure that they are, and you'll all have a happier, healthier, and more fulfilled life.

Whoever finds a friend, finds a treasure.

—Italian proverb

CHAPTER 7
LA FAMIGLIA (FAMILY)

SACRIFICES AND LEGACIES

"Take-a me now, Jesus! Take-a me now!"

That would be my grandmother's cry at every holiday dinner. You see, we'd already eaten more than a human should consume in one (or three!) sittings. There simply was no more room. We tried to decline as Grandma encouraged us to "have-a some more". That's when she'd invoke divine intervention because, in her guilt-inducing broken English, Grandma exclaimed to the Heavens, "They no like-a my cooking! I'm a failure!"

You guessed it: we had-a some more!

In my family, food is love, and our grandmother knew how to express it! For Thanksgiving, she'd make the traditional American feast, and she'd add—not substitute—Italian holiday specialties. Christmas and Easter were all-day affairs starting with church and continuing into the evening as aunts, uncles, and cousins stopped by for coffee and conversation.

I remember Grandma bustling around the kitchen, even when she used a wheelchair during the last decade of her life. It still amazes me how she did everything so well and never once complained. Sundays meant sausage and meatballs simmering in the sauce she made from the tomatoes they'd picked over the summer. Before the holidays, even the bedrooms and hallways became storage for baked goods. Love was in the air!

It's not just about the food. It's about what happens *around* the food: cherished ones are together, laughing and sometimes yelling, weaving together the familial ties. At the table, we listen and hear tales of the past, share stories of overcoming today's struggles, and offer sage advice for tomorrow.

As author and motivational speaker Leo Buscaglia said, "All of my youth, growing up in my Italian family, was focused around the table. That's where I learned about love."

Studies confirm the importance of family dinners. Columbia University reports that teens who eat meals with their parents not only report having high-quality relationships, and are much less likely to use drugs and alcohol.[1]

My brother Keith and I were fortunate to grow up across the street from our grandparents. By spending so much time with them, their everyday lives became our lessons. They didn't realize they were teaching us the importance of a strong work ethic, how to interact with others, and the value of family, friends, and faith. They were the masters and we were the apprentices in the trade of life.

RESPECT

First and foremost, we were taught to honor and respect others, especially our elders and authority figures. That meant giving up our seat, saying "please" and "thank you," and dressing appropriately when going to church, school, or to someone's house.

We pitched in whenever we were asked, whether it was helping Grandma to hang curtains or driving Grandpa to a doctor's appointment. These acts of service weren't done because we *had* to, but because we were honored to give back—no matter how minutely—to those who'd done so much for us.

At a recent event in the "Little Italy" area of Providence, RI, the Mattera legacy was honored. A plaque was unveiled that told the story of my great-great uncle's journey of achieving his American dream of becoming a successful entrepreneur. My cousin Linda wisely remarked that we (the children and grandchildren) are who we are today because of our parents' and grandparents' sacrifices and God's grace. Let's never forget that.

In a related note, *Mamma* will always claim the highest priority for most Italian and Italian-American men. If you are the sweetheart of such a man, recognize that fact. Even if you think he shows his mother too much attention, it's best not to verbalize that if you want to preserve your relationship with either of them.

Mamma mia! I can foresee the hate mail I'm going to get for saying that! Is it right or wrong for your Italian stallion to esteem his mother so highly? That's up to you to decide. Remember, though, that he's teaching your children how to respect their mother and women in general. Is that so bad?

REPUTATION

Did you know that you're an Ambassador? Well, you are! Any time you go to work or a store or post a comment, you're representing your family. Is that fair? No, but it's true.

Think about it: have you ever questioned someone's upbringing based on his behavior? You probably never met his parents, but you're surprised that he never learned proper etiquette.

Having a good reputation isn't about putting on a false façade. It's about presenting our best selves because we make an impression, good or bad, every time we step out of the house. Again, it's not necessarily fair, but that's how we humans act.

This will be discussed in detail in chapter nine *La bella figura*.

FAITH

Early on Sunday mornings, we'd often go to church with our grandparents for the Italian service. No, we kids didn't understand a word, but we realized the importance of this weekly ritual. We also felt special because, when we returned home, we had what the grown-ups had with breakfast: *espresso*—which was a drop of coffee with a lot of milk for us.

Most Italians and Italian-Americans have a strong belief in God. This was instilled in us from birth. No matter your religion, there is comfort, peace and hope when you have faith in a higher power.

I'm not going to debate whether or not God is real or which religion is best. I will say that I've witnessed so many miracles in my life that I believe someone watches over us.

Faith doesn't shield you from the storms of life. It's the life preserver in the storm. The beliefs that were passed on are reminders that every test will eventually bring a testimony, and that there's always hope.

FRACTURED FAMILIES

Sadly, not all family members hold the same values as we do. For whatever reason, they place material gain over loyalty and selfishness over love. I've experienced this in my own family and witnessed it in too many others. Often, when a relative who had money passes away, true colors become evident.

I won't go into details about the sad saga of my family's split. Just because something is true doesn't protect me from libel!

In my opinion, this happened because the heads of the families allowed it. If my grandparents were alive, the rift that divided the Matteras would've been halted as soon as it started. However, as our codes of conduct and honor became more diluted over time, the importance of family isn't what it once was.

Yes, I attempted to rectify the situation several times. However, the tentacles of greed were too deep in the hearts of the troublemakers. It took me a long time to finally accept what happened and to move forward from there.

Perhaps you can learn from my family's misfortune. If you're the elder of your clan, be vigilant to encourage—maybe even demand—loyalty, respect, and selflessness. No matter what your status in the family, don't cause division, gossip, or force people to take sides. Be the light and not an accomplice to the darkness.

FINDING FAMILIES

In recent years, there's been a buzz about having your DNA tested to identify your ancestral heritage. There have been funny stories and shocking surprises that have made the news.

Of course, the old fashioned method of tracing your roots is to gather documents and interview people who may have known your great-grandparents. I prefer this approach because there are usually tales and photos of these once-living pieces of our historical puzzle.

Several excellent websites can help you draw the branches of your family tree. It's fascinating to see the ship manifests and other documents that fill in the blanks of stories we've heard. As these sites grow, and more people input data, the task becomes easier.

Just a few years ago, I had an *a-ha!* moment when I thought to check *Italian* genealogical websites. Why didn't I think of that before? This research told more of the story: my grandfather's side of the family (Mattera) came from Greece centuries ago. I already knew that, and you can see Greek architecture on the island of Ischia. However, I didn't know that they lived in the southern town of Matera, Italy, well before settling on the island. My long-time question of the etymology of my surname was finally answered. (Yes, the single "t" doubled over time.) Previously, I thought my last name was some variation of the word *matto*, which means "crazy" in Italian. It wouldn't have surprised me if that was indeed the meaning!

The Italian family tree websites also led to the long-ago origins of my grandmother's ancestors (Iacono). They came to Ischia from Spain, probably Catalonia. Could that be why I felt so comfortable and connected when we visited Barcelona? Perhaps. No matter what, I find it fascinating to imagine and appreciate my ancestors' journeys to where we are today.

If you have any older family members or neighbors, ask them about yesteryear. I'd even encourage you to record their responses. Not only will you discover a depth of understanding your roots, you'll show that person that their memories are valuable. That's a win-win.

In my case, it was relatively (pun intended) easy to find my Italian families. My Uncle Johnny, who spoke the dialect, called his cousins on Ischia several times a year. During our first trip there, though, it hit me that our family's link across the ocean was only one person. I didn't want to be someone who says, "Oh, we have family in Europe, but we lost touch." Why would anyone let such a treasure drift out of their life?

Knowing that the language was the biggest barrier to truly getting to know my Italian family, I started taking group lessons once a week. (I was almost 40 at the time, by the way.) About a year later, I lived in Florence, Italy, for two months to attend a language school.

Am I saying that you must learn the language of your ancestors? No. It would be helpful, but not necessary, especially with all the electronic translators we have today. Further, English is the language of business. So, it's spoken—or, at least understood—in many countries' larger cities. However, I feel that my experiences in Italy are richer because I can communicate in the mother tongue. This is more noticeable when your relatives are in smaller towns.

My partner, Bob, grew up hearing about the small town in Italy where his grandfather was born. However, any connections to those relatives were lost decades ago. A few years ago, Bob expressed interest in finding his ancestral town. We knew the Corsi family came from some place called "San Michele." Do you know how many San Micheles there are in Italy? A lot! It took some detective work to find the needle in the haystack.

We explored a small shred of evidence of the Corsi forefathers: Bob's cousin Lisa had a copy of a photo of the family's tombstone. On that paper, we saw the name "San Michele in

Teverina." Ta-da! We found it on the map and planned how to get there during our next trip.

In the meantime, I looked in the *Pagine Bianche* (White Pages) for any Corsi listings; there were only three and included a mechanic. We found that humorous since Bob is a master mechanic.

When we arrived in San Michele, the hotel owner called the Corsi families. Alas, none of them claimed to have any American relatives. As we drove around the town, we asked people if they knew any of Bob's family, past or present. No one did...supposedly. (We'll loop back to this in a moment.) This was a perfect example of how speaking the language was valuable; no one we encountered knew English.

The hotel owner took us to City Hall where we met Marilena. She made copies of the birth certificates of Bob's grandfather and great-grandfather. When we picked up the documents later that day, she offered to take us to see the original Corsi home. Wow! We later discovered that Marilena and Bob are distant cousins through marriage.

As we drove up the street that we had been on the day before, Marilena stopped to talk to one of the men that we had already met. Come to find out, not only did this man know of Bob's family, he was living in the original Corsi home!

You might be saying, "What the bleep? That guy lied to you!" Let's look at it from his point of view. If some strangers stopped you, out of the blue, and asked if you knew someone, wouldn't you be wary?

When I went to Ischia the first time, with my father and Uncle Johnny, we ran into a similar situation. While most of our family welcomed us with open arms, one cousin was skeptical of our visit. He thought that we were there to reclaim Grandpa's land that was given to other cousins decades ago. Once he realized that our motives were pure, he let down his guard.

I tell you all this so you're aware of how your new-found family might interpret your sudden interest in them. Don't inquire about houses or land; let them bring up that topic. Ask them about the closest relatives that you have in common. Bring old photos; they may spark a memory or two. You might even show them a family tree and ask for their help with it.

Remember the mechanic from San Michele's White Pages? By chance, we met him at the town's cemetery. Bob and I were cleaning the Corsi family tomb and placing flowers in the urns. A man walked by and asked why we were there. Pointing to the name at the top of the tomb, I explained that Bob was the great-great-grandson of Luigi Corsi. His face lit up as he exclaimed that we were related; he was the mechanic, Fulvio.

He proceeded to take us around the cemetery and "introduced" us to his loved ones who were there, resting in peace. From that chance meeting, we've since spent time with them on subsequent visits, and we stay in touch throughout the year.

Your take-away from that story is to inspire you to get out there rather than hole up in your hotel room. Spend time in the coffee shops, piazzas, and even cemeteries. You may feel awkward as everyone wonders who these *stranieri* (strangers) are. Smile and strike up a conversation. You never know who's walking by you.

One more tidbit about tracing your roots in the old country: street names may have changed since Great-grandpa lived there, especially after World War II. Bob's father tried to find the Corsi home when he stationed in Italy in the 1950's. When he asked locals about the street his father had mentioned, everyone said it didn't exist. Today, there's a plaque on that street that shows the history of this name change.

Further, Bob's grandfather's birth certificate had a neighborhood name as the place of where he was born. Only someone who lived in that area would know where that was. A lifelong resident, Marilena knew the exact location.

In the search for your ancestry, be persistent. You'll encounter road blocks, and go down the wrong path at times. Channel your inner Inspector Montalbano (a modern-day detective TV series in Italy) and look for the clues to your past. It'll be worth it!

FAMILY FOREVER

When I think about my parents and grandparents, I'm sad that my nieces and nephews will never know them. It could even be more depressing to think that they could be forgotten in one more generation. However, we can prevent their stories from vanishing into oblivion.

This is one reason that the traditional Sunday dinner is so important. As we pass that side dish that Grandma always made, we can talk about her. The person now seated at the head of the table can share stories about how Grandpa ruled his small kingdom from there. Use the dishes and coffee cups to remember loved ones who've passed, and be sure to tell others about them.

I often sign my letters, emails, and book inscriptions with "*Tante belle cose,*" which English speakers could interpret as "Many blessings." I started doing this after being with my *Zio Michele* (Uncle Mike) in Italy. Every time we would part, he'd kiss me twice and say, "*Tante belle cose.*"

Uncle Mike's words were filled with so much that couldn't be expressed: he wanted the best for the family and me in America, and we were grateful to be together. As the last surviving sibling of my grandmother, I was honored and blessed to know this kind, hard-working, and loving man who always had a twinkle in his eye.

Five minutes ago, you knew nothing of Michele Iacono of Ischia, but now you do. That's the power of talking about our loved ones. That's how we keep their stories alive and relevant to the next generation.

Aside from Sunday dinners, here are some other ways to keep the family flame burning:

❖ Celebrate someone's *onomastico* (name day)—in Italy, your name day is like a second birthday, and who doesn't like presents? For example, Saint John's Day is June 24th. So, Uncle Johnny got some extra love that day. My father, Joe, made sure everyone knew when it was Saint Joseph's Day! It's a tradition to enjoy one of the delectable pastries of the day (*zeppole di San Giuseppe*), and it's also Fathers' Day in Italy. Tell the younger generation about your ancestor on his or her *onomastico*.

❖ Family Friday—Find a photo from the past. Post it online or email it to your siblings, children, nieces and nephews with names, the date and the story behind the shot.

❖ Create a video or scrapbook of your family's history. Include maps, ship manifests, birth and marriage certificates, and—most important—photographs. It doesn't have to be perfect; just do it with love.

It's been said that the family is the building block of society. I believe that the relationship between these families is the cement. My grandfather Ignazio was a concrete mason, and he'd likely agree. By caring for our families and reaching out to others, we can live in a strong fortress that will withstand any storm that life may send our way.

I know for certain that we never lose the people we love, even to death. They continue to participate in every act, thought and decision we make. Their love leaves an indelible imprint in our memories. We find comfort in knowing that our lives have been enriched by having shared their love.

—Leo Buscaglia

Chapter 8
Amore (Love)

The star in my sky

Wanted: single male who is intelligent, trustworthy, passionate, understanding, loving, adventurous, and funny. Hairy chest would be nice.

When I described Mr. Right to my friends, several thought I was looking for a dog! (Actually, that was Plan B.) However, I did find true love with a human that checked off all those canine boxes. Yes, there were a few frogs that I had to kiss first; I'll get to that later in this chapter.

Everlasting Love

When I look at photographs of my grandparents, I see a depth of love that stood strongly whether there were troubles or tranquility, loss or laughter. Married for well over 60 years, they were more in love with each passing decade.

To my knowledge, none of us ever asked our grandparents for marriage advice. We didn't have to; they lived it. Everything they did, whether it was Grandpa going to work or Grandma canning vegetables, all was done out of love for each other and the family. They both contributed and appreciated each other.

Sure, they had arguments. That's when the volume went from loud to thunderous, and they spoke in their native dialect. Mind you, they didn't hide behind closed doors for this, and I'm glad they didn't. You see, we learned even how to disagree with our partners: you get it out in the open, discuss it, decide, and then go back to where you took a detour. You don't hold grudges against the people that you love.

After our grandparents passed, we found postcards that Grandpa had sent to Grandma while she was still in Italy. Even though they were an ocean apart, that didn't stop Grandpa from courting his beloved. We never knew that Grandpa was such a romantic! He called her the star of his sky, the beat of his heart. (It's okay to sigh here!) Even into their twilight years, she was still his star and his heartbeat.

I once asked my father's best friend, David, what the key was to his long and happy marriage. He said that they do everything together. To clarify, he went on to say that any event he goes to, she's welcome to attend, and vice versa. He probably doesn't want to go shopping with the girls, but he isn't forbidden to join them. Further, they make it a point to pursue activities that they both enjoy, like karaoke.

My partner, Bob, and I do this, too. We both love to travel, go to concerts, and ride the Harley. At the same time, I'm happy that he goes to a heavy equipment auction with his friends, and he's fine with me meeting my girlfriends for dinner. The key is that we spend the majority of our free time doing things together. I'm poignantly aware of this since I believe that one cause of my divorce was that we drifted apart by *not* pursuing common interests.

Another crucial aspect of a relationship—romantic or not—is to understand the other person's Love Language[1]. Written by Gary Chapman, his series of books are practical and eye-opening about how we give and receive love. Mr. Chapman should be made an honorary Italian for his work on the topic of *amore*!

To summarize, we each have a primary Love Language that we understand. Think of it this way: if someone said that they loved you in Martian, you wouldn't get it. Their intention was noble, but the message wasn't received. If someone keeps giving you gifts to show affection, that's nice, but you may feel loved by spending time together.

Be sure to express your love every day, in words and actions, whether you're in the same house or separated by miles. Never stop courting your sweetheart.

LATIN LOVERS

It's February 14th as I'm writing this chapter. Italian-American social media groups are posting things like, "Valentines' Day is for amateurs…Italians are lovers every day!" After all, the word "romance" does have its root in Rome. So, there may be some truth to the stereotypical Latin lover.

When I was single and traveling to Italy alone, they were everywhere. It was certainly good for my heart-broken ego to have the attention of those Mediterranean mavericks. It seems that Italian men embellish the famous Descartes' quote: "I think I am sexy, therefore I am."

Latin Lover Lesson One is to believe that you are lovable. This doesn't mean that you must have a smokin' hot body, a fancy car or a huge bank account. It means that you're mature enough and confident enough to understand that a meaningful relationship is two-sided. You have a lot to offer, and your sweetheart will, too. If you lack self-confidence, feel free to jump ahead to chapter eleven.

Latin Lover Lesson Two is always to look your best when in public. Italians have elegance and style even when they're wearing jeans. They have a keen fashion sense, and the importance of making a good impression is ingrained in us. More on this in chapter nine—*La Bella Figura*.

You might be thinking that we shouldn't judge a book by its cover. Yet, in the Library of Life, the attractive dust jacket gets our attention, and we want to take it home and dive into the pages. Wait, are we still talking about books?

Seriously, dressing appropriately and looking classy sends a message to others that you're respectful and thoughtful. What a breath of fresh air in this narcissistic world! That will surely make you stand out like *cannoli* in a box of donuts!

LOOKING FOR LOVE

Many people are surprised that I met my partner, Bob, online. At the time, I'd recently moved back to Rhode Island, had a home-based office, and wasn't a fan of going to night clubs. So, unless I had a crush on the mailman, I needed a way to find companionship.

Of course, the techniques in the chapter about friendship can be useful to find romance, too. In fact, meeting people with whom you share common interests is the best foundation for love.

Since love interests weren't appearing within my social circles, I enrolled in a dating website. After uploading some photos and posting my profile, the adventure began. At first, the instant attention was flattering. Then, it became a bit overwhelming. It felt like an internet meat market, and I was the newest slab of prime rib.

Overall, it wasn't a terrible experience. Even though there were a couple of creeps that contacted me via the website's messenger, anyone I met in person was genuinely nice, even the accountant who liked to vacation at nudist camps. (Nope, not for me!)

One of my friends also tried online dating and had a strange experience. He went to meet a woman in the food court at the mall. Once there, he saw two women sitting on a bench; one of them looked like the picture from the website.

My friend approached the one he thought was his date and asked, "Are you Maria?" She pointed to the woman beside her. My friend was confused because the pointing woman looked like the photo. Maria explained that her sister was much more attractive, so she used her picture instead of her own!

If you do try online dating, please be honest right from the start! Photos should be no more than a year old, they should be of *you*! For heaven's sake, be sure to crop out former lovers. Have a trusted friend review your profile; they'll likely suggest adding attributes that you take for granted about yourself.

Always remember that you can't force a relationship into existence. What I mean is that you need to relax and trust that you'll meet someone. If we have an air of desperation, we'll repel people rather than attract them. Simply go about your life with optimism and the lessons from this book. It's only a matter of time for Cupid to put your heart in line with another.

I'm stressing the positive outlook because of a story about a lost love connection. Anna is beautiful, intelligent and kind. Like many, she tried online dating. However, she had a series of bad experiences. One guy even excused himself to go to the rest-room while at a restaurant but never returned. Anna was losing hope with the entire process.

Making yet another attempt at a love connection, she agreed to meet a new online Romeo at a coffee shop. He was polite, well-spoken and neatly dressed. He was the perfect guy! However, Anna was sobbing as she told the tale of their date.

You see, she fully expected Romeo to be like all the others she had met. She was tired of kissing frogs and getting warts instead of a prince. She planned to meet him after a jog in the park. Doubting that this could be Mr. Right, she didn't bother taking a shower or even to brush her hair. She was so embarrassed and disappointed in herself that she abruptly fled the café after a short time.

If Anna had even a glimmer of hope for a Hallmark movie ending, she surely would've presented her best self. Instead, she gave in to the understandable discouragement and showed up half-heartedly. She expected the date to go poorly, and that prophecy was self-fulfilled.

A story where they all live happily ever after is how Sophia Loren met the love of her life, film producer Carlo Ponti. She went to a restaurant where they happened to be having a beauty pageant. Carlo, much older than Sophia, saw her and encouraged her to participate. From there, he cast her in movies, they fell in love and were eventually married. Just think if she stayed home that night instead of going to the restaurant. Sophia's life would likely have been quite different.

The lesson is to be ready for love. You never know when that casual remark in the produce section or pouring some coffee at your cousin's party could be the beginning of a romance. I'm not saying that you need to wear your Sunday best to the grocery store. The most important thing to wear is your smile, along with a dash of confidence. Expect the best and it will eventually occur.

GETTING TO KNOW MR. (OR MS.) RIGHT

I'd just returned from another solo trip to Italy. This time, though, I finally felt the desire to have someone with me the next time. Before leaving the states, I took myself off the dating website. A few days after coming home, I made my profile active once again.

The next day, a cute guy "winked" at me, and I "winked" back. We then exchanged phone numbers and he called. Bob and I planned to meet the next evening for pizza. (You know: when the moon hits your eye like a big pizza pie.[2] We must have subconsciously planned it that way!)

We met at a charming place in the Little Italy area of Providence. From there, we took a stroll and ended up at a coffee shop. There, we shared a dessert and (musical crescendo goes here!) our first kiss.

Our second date was two days later. From that Saturday, we have been together every day since, except for work-related trips.

I share our story not to boast, but to give you hope. We were both divorced and pushing 50 when we met. We had our share of heartbreak and tragedies, all of which made us keenly aware of what we wanted and didn't want in a relationship.

Was it worth the wait? Absolutely. Do we wish we had met sooner? Yes and no. Of course, more years together would've been wonderful. However, our experiences and how we respond to them make us who we are. I wouldn't be the person I am today without them. I had some critical lessons to learn before meeting my life partner. Therefore, I choose to believe that Bob and I met at exactly the right time.

As you get to know your possible soul mate, watch actions more than just listening to words. We all are on our best behavior when we first meet someone. Over time, you'll see this person in different situations that reveal his or her true self.

Look for red flags like explosions of anger for minor occurrences. For example, the man I dated before I met Bob flew into a rage when I made a mistake about which highway exit to take. At the time, I brushed it off to him being tired. If something like that happens rarely, it's probably nothing. However, if that behavior is the rule rather than the exception, tread cautiously.

Other warning signs in matters of love are the same as we addressed in the chapter about friends. Review the section there called Remodeling Your Belltower.

Be careful of what you tolerate, too, because you're teaching people how to treat you. Sadly, some will try to make you feel inferior or pretend to be joking when they say or do something hurtful. If you're afraid to address any disrespect, that's a sign that this may not be the best relationship for you.

I realize that many of you may fear you'll get hurt once again. We're slow to trust, and it's wise to be careful. I hope you don't let mistrust from the past tarnish your view of today. Just because your ex was unfaithful, that doesn't mean your new love will be. In other words, it's not fair for one person to pay for the sins of another.

At the same time, don't blindly accept someone too soon. This is especially important if you've been lonely or sad for a while. We might be so caught up in the excitement that we don't see the caution light flashing.

How do we learn to trust someone, then? There are three tests:

1) Do they do what they say?

2) Are they open and honest?

3) Do they take responsibility for their mistakes?

If a person passes all three, the light turns green and you continue down the *Via Del'amore* (Lovers' Lane).

FANNING THE FLAME

Earlier in this chapter, I gave two principles of keeping love alive: spending time together and never stop courting your sweetheart.

One way to do both is to commit to doing something together each year that you'll talk about for the rest of your lives. It could be as grand as an amazing vacation or as simple as sleeping in a tent in the backyard one night. It doesn't even have to be necessarily fun. For example, Bob and I worked an entire summer, several days a week, on a monstrous project at my house. Trust me, we don't relive that memory with joy, but it was a mountain that we scaled together.

The purpose is to strengthen your partnership by weaving these events into your love story. As time progresses, you write more chapters that are titled, "Remember when we...?" Making memories together creates closeness.

I realize there are times when you don't want to spend your precious time doing something that doesn't interest you. Perhaps you've been invited to dinner by your in-laws who are experts at underhanded insults. You'd rather put pineapple on your pizza—we've already addressed the horror of that!—than be with *those* people.

My wise friend Holly once told me, "If it's important to Bob, it's important to you." Of course, she's right. There are times when we must channel our inner *bella figura* and act accordingly. It's not a matter of giving in or being forced. Rather, you're honoring and respecting your partner. After all, love is an action.

Forgiveness is paramount in any relationship, especially intimate ones. As mere mortals, we will fall. Choosing to pardon our partners is one of the highest expressions of love and grace. Yes, some sins are mortal, and some affect your children. Each case is different, and you need to prayerfully decide which course to take.

Please consider a quote by one of my favorite authors, Max Lucado. He said, "Relationships don't thrive because the guilty are punished but because the innocent are merciful." I hope that you can extend grace and salvage what remains.

If your partner wants to end the relationship, or you must escape for fear of abuse, remember what one of my friends, Paul, told me when I was getting divorced: "It may be the end of the chapter, but it's not the end of the book." I should embroider that on a pillow!

Another key to a blissful relationship is communication. In addition to knowing how to speak your partner's Love Language, it's important to address any friction sooner rather than later.[1] Even the Bible tells us to not go to bed if we're angry. A minor infraction can evolve into a wedge that splits your once happy home.

To give you an example, my father ate an apple almost every day. He'd wash it off at the sink, and then pull off the stem. Instead of throwing it away, he just left it on the counter. This irritated my mother beyond belief. She'd let them pile up and finally throw them in the trash. At one point, she stuck them to a piece of tape dangling from the cupboard like flypaper.

I don't know why my father pretended not to see my mother's attempts at changing his behavior. (Really, how can you miss a string of apple stems hanging there?) I do know that my mother's reaction didn't help. She was angry, and, therefore, unable to give or receive the full measure of love.

Maybe your sweetie doesn't have a fruit fixation, but perhaps they never put their dirty clothes in the hamper or put the seat down. Arrggh! Frustrating, isn't it? I'm not saying that it's okay to do things that cause friction. Instead, I encourage you to check your attitude.

For one thing, who says that you *have* to put the cap back on the toothpaste? Is there a law? I agree that there should be, but there's not. We don't like it when someone tells us, "It's my way or the highway!" Let's not make the same demand when it's not something vitally important.

Plus, how do we feel when that darned seat is up *again*? We clench our teeth and squint our eyes. Do you think your honey wants a kiss from that? Heck, no! We're letting something insignificant chip away at our frame of mind.

A better way to handle these bothersome incidents is logically and without drama. We can simply say, "Oh, you left the empty milk carton on the counter." That's it; end of story! You got it off your chest, and now you get to choose the direction from there. I hope you take the higher road and let go of any emotion that's attached to that carton.

Your partner may never put the cap on the toothpaste. Yet, because you're a caring and reasonable person, you decide not to let a piece of plastic be the starting point to divorce. As my cousin Linda has asked me when I've whined to her about something, "Is it a deal-breaker?"

What can you do if your sweetheart is mad? Try putting a towel over his shoulders like a cape. Then say, "Now you're *super* mad!" I'm sure that will break the tension, and you'll both laugh and laugh. Sorry, I can't keep a straight face with that one. I'm kidding! Do *not* do that! We both know that won't end well, and someone's sleeping on the couch!

All joking aside, I do have one secret to share with the ladies about communication. Have you ever suggested an ideal solution to a problem and your man ignored or rejected it? That's because our guys always want to appear as strong and intelligent leaders. For us to make a suggestion may be hurtful because they feel that *they* should have thought of it.

The key to offering an idea is how you present it. Are you ready for the magical phrase? Start your proposal by saying, "I know you already thought of this…" Boom! You shared your perfect idea, and he kept his crown straight. And, we all live happily ever after.

You're welcome!

* * *

No matter what phase of love you're in right now, you choose how you respond. If you're lonely and looking, keep living a life that brings you a sense of fulfillment. Even if you never find Mr. or Mrs. Right, your life will be beautiful because you made it that way.

There may be some of you who feel stuck in a relationship. I can't tell you to stay or leave. I chose to remain in a loveless marriage because I made a vow. However, if there is any hint of abuse to you or your children, I'd tell you to make a plan to get out of there!

My wish is that you can find reconciliation. However, I know that it's not always possible. If that happens, don't let the judgmental jackals tear apart your self-esteem. They don't know the whole story, and you don't need people like that in your life. Move forward from here, my friend!

For those of us blessed to have a life partner, let's keep the flames burning by courting our sweethearts each day. There will be times when we say, "I love you more than yesterday—because yesterday, you really ticked me off!" Forgiveness and grace, mixed with love and a little adventure, will keep us together.

In that book which is my memory, on the first page—that is the chapter when I first met you— appear the words, "Here begins a new life."

—Dante Alighieri

CHAPTER 9
LA BELLA FIGURA

WANT TO CHANGE THE WORLD?
SAY THE MAGIC WORD!

Have you ever been cut off while driving or held the door for someone who didn't even acknowledge you? Or maybe you have a friend or relative who is always, always late. Sadly, that's the state of our world today. Too many people are so rushed, stressed, and—dare I say it?—self-centered to be kind to each other.

Wouldn't it be nice if people were just, well, nice? Here is where this ever-present Italian concept makes a subtle but powerful entrance.

The phrase *la bella figura* has two meanings. The literal translation is "a beautiful figure" which alludes to looking our best. At the same time, it goes beyond the figurative interpretation of "a good impression." It's a way of life that brings civility and even hope back to our society.

This attitude in living also prevents us from being victims of circumstances. How? Glad you asked! We've all said something like, "That makes me so mad!" Yet, nothing can *make* us angry, sad, upset, etc. without us allowing it. We choose how we respond. When we say that something makes us feel a certain way, we give it power and feel like victims. Instead, deciding to act with a *bella figura*, we have jurisdiction over the one thing we do control: ourselves. That realization can release you from victim mentality and move on to creating a life that you love.

As I'm writing this chapter in April 2020, the world is on edge and Italy in lockdown. Instead of wrestling over toilet paper and hoarding hand sanitizer, the Italians are singing from their balconies together. Their culture of double-kiss greetings and being surrounded by family and friends is a poignant memory. Yet, the country's cry is *#andratuttobene,* which means "everything will be alright."

Aside from the perpetual hope that most Italians possess during this crisis, they wouldn't fight in a grocery store because it's childish, rude, and inappropriate. It's the polar opposite of a *bella figura.* They also remember their country's history of overcoming far worse situations. Whereas, in America, we haven't faced anything like this in decades. Still, that doesn't justify our embarrassing behavior.

For most of us of Italian heritage, the *bella figura* was a constant theme in our homes. It was taught in the classroom of life by our elders; thus, another important reason to spend time with family. Even when we disagree with someone, this attitude guides us to listen and consider another person's perspective. They may not change our minds, but we won't become insulting or mean… at least not in public! If you must say something harsh, say it in Italian, and with a smile. It sounds so much nicer that way!

Don't worry if this lifestyle concept wasn't a high priority in your formative years. It's a skill, and that means it can be learned. In this chapter, we'll look at the various aspects of *la bella figura.* Then, instead of spiraling into a close-minded and hostile abyss, we can spark a kinder and more beautiful world.

LA BELLA FIGURA: PART 1—APPEARANCE

We all know the saying about not judging a book by its cover. However, you and I do this every day. In mere seconds, we form an opinion about someone based on his or her clothing, posture and facial expressions; that's before even a word is spoken!

If you're rolling your eyeballs about this section because you feel it's superficial, consider my perspective. It's not about looking better than others, pretending to be something we're not, or spending money to stay on top of trends. *La bella figura* is about being authentic, appropriate and more. Let me explain.

Have you ever worn a pair of jeans or shoes that were too tight? You probably couldn't wait to get home and put on something comfortable. Have you ever attended a special event and realized that your zipper was broken? Ugh.

In situations like those, we tend to develop a case of ingrown eyeballs. What? You see, we're so busy fidgeting with our clothing or apologizing for our appearance that we don't truly pay attention to other people. Instead, we're concentrating on ourselves, looking inward.

By dressing appropriately for a situation, and in a manner that flatters your physique, you feel good about yourself. Then, you can forget about yourself and focus on others. Therefore, it's not self-centered to want to look your best.

Further, if you want to make a difference in the world, your appearance is part of your "marketing". More people will hear your message if you dress the part. If I taught a class on making meatballs while wearing scuba gear, many students would be confused. Yet, if I traded the wetsuit for an apron, that would make sense with my lesson. Granted, you may use incongruity to get attention, but we're talking about appealing to a wider audience. So, dress the part, and they'll listen intently to your words.

By the way, I do make great meatballs. But I digress.

Did you know that how you're dressed can affect your performance? Yes, we can all agree that wearing dress shoes aren't the best choice to play tennis. It goes further than that with a concept called Enclothed Cognition[1].

A study conducted by two professors from Northwestern University showed how a simple coat increased test results. One group of people heard the white coat was a doctor's, and the other group thought it was for a painter. The group wearing the doctor's lab coat performed better on a test than those wearing a painter's smock.

This suggests that it's not the actual article of clothing but the association we make with it. That's good news for you and for your wallet. We may not be able to afford a designer wardrobe, but we can all choose clothing that makes us confident. No ingrown eyeballs, either.

I'd like to make one more point about how wanting to look your best is not superficial. Imagine that everyone around you dressed in grey. Children were riding their grey bikes, and the grey tulips were in bloom. We wouldn't want to stay in Greyville very long, would we?

On the other hand, how do you feel when you see a young-ster wearing a yellow shirt and neon green tennis shoes? When you see your sweetheart dressed up for a wedding, you probably think, *Mamma mia!*

Likewise, when people look at us, we can affect their view of the world. No, my ensemble might not change anything, but it may bring a smile. Further, beauty begets beauty. In other words, people in your day-to-day life will likewise be encouraged to step up their style game.

We also tend to behave better when we're well dressed. We stand tall in that suit, and we tend to exhibit good manners. On the flip side, we let down our guard (and, often inhibitions) when we're dressed more casually. There's nothing wrong with that when we're with family and friends. When we're out of the house, though, we put our best foot forward.

Let's take this idea just one step further. What if we all made a small effort to dress not only for ourselves but also with the thought of positively influencing our surroundings? Our society would be full of people who give a d*mn. That, my friend, is one powerful effect of *la bella figura.*

STYLE AND SUSTAINABILITY

Whenever I go shopping with my Italian cousins, I inwardly gasp when I see how much they spend on one pair of slacks or a shirt. However, that item is beautifully made, fits them perfectly, and will last for years. They feel confident when wearing it which frees them to be themselves.

Instead of having a closet full of clothes and *nothing to wear*, we can curate a wardrobe that suits our lifestyles and make it simpler to get dressed each day. That saves time and money in the long run. Further, there will be less waste because you won't be tossing out those things—with price tags still attached—that you never wear.

My recommendation is to buy the best basic pieces (slacks, blazers, etc.) that you can afford. You can mix and match those with less-expensive items like shirts and sweaters. Before you buy yet another article of clothing, ask yourself if it will go with what you already own. Also, will you need to purchase other things so you can wear it? For example, that jacket might be fabulous, but do you need a top, special undergarments, or different slacks to complete the look?

As for fashion, adding one or two pieces in a season will keep your look up-to-date. I like to incorporate trends into my wardrobe through accessories. Last year's coat looks fresh with a colorful scarf, and a basic jeans-and-shirt combo becomes an outfit with a great belt and statement earrings.

Speaking of belts and earrings, I developed a class years ago called *The ABCs of Accessorizing*. It's an effortless way to elevate your look.

Accent – Add an accent color to your outfit, like adding red to your black slacks and white shirt. It's pleasing to the eye to stick with odd numbers. That could mean one red jacket, or a red belt, necklace, and lipstick (three spots of color).

Bottom to top – Bring the bottom color to the top. Using the basic outfit in the previous example, add a black scarf or tie. I wouldn't suggest black lipstick unless your style is Goth.

Creativity – Think outside the jewelry box! Why not use that long necklace or a tie as a belt? Learn interesting ways to wear the scarf that you bought on vacation. Layer necklaces or pin several vintage brooches on your lapel or handbag.

I'll bet you already have accessories to make your own ABCs. Have fun with it! You might even do this with a friend. We tend to see possibilities with someone else's collection easier than we do with our own, and they'll do the same for you.

When we use what we already have and buy clothing from a perspective of quality instead of quantity, we feel better about our closets. That's because we're being good stewards of our hard-earned money and not being wasteful. Knowing that we look darn good is a sweet perk!

One of my favorite Vloggers on the subject of sustainable style is Alyssa Beltempo. Her slogan of "More Creativity, Less Consumption" rings true with her shop-your-closet and wearable trend weekly videos.

STYLE AND SELF-AWARENESS

It's important to build your *bella figura* wardrobe around your real and current life. For instance, I don't need a dozen suits since I don't work in corporate America any longer. Yes, I still have two for those rare occasions when that's the dress code. I also have a couple of after-five items; I don't want to be rushed and stressed looking for something like that! Yet the majority of my clothing is suitable for my business-casual workweek and relaxed leisure time.

Do you know those little tags with numbers inside clothing? It's crazy how much emphasis we put on what size we wear. Please look at sizes as general suggestions. I once bought three dresses (due to a job change) in the same store; they were three different sizes. Instead of that menacing number, concentrate on the fit. Too loose can be as unflattering as too tight.

As you hone your style, there are numerous online resources available such as videos and blogs. Many stylists offer complementary courses. As you search the web, enter terms that match your objective. Try something like "elegant work wardrobe women" or "business casual men". Pay attention to *why* you're drawn to certain looks: is it the color, shape, or vibe? You'll start to see a pattern. For example, you may be drawn to neutrals with pops of bright hues, and structured rather than loose fits.

The internet is also an instrument to learn how to use what you already own. Perhaps you have a shirt that you love, but you're not sure how to wear it. Look online for images with a description of that shirt. Include terms like "street style" or "outfit ideas" for inspiration.

Italians seem to have an inborn sense of style. They make jeans and a t-shirt look chic and sexy. I still have yet to figure out how the women can walk on cobblestone streets in stilettos. I guess I'll just have to keep going to Italy to conduct more research!

LA BELLA FIGURA: PART 2—THE TRUE ITALIAN CULTURE

Many people who live outside of Italy have a stereotypical view of its people. The entertainment industry paints a picture of loud and conniving gangsters who drive Cadillacs. "Italian" restaurants serve meatballs and spaghetti on the same plate or—worse—put pineapple on a pizza. If you didn't cringe at that sentence, you may have fallen victim to Hollywood's portrayal of my ethnic heritage.

However, a defining characteristic of Italians is *la bella figura*. Going beyond reputation, it's about honor and respect for yourself and others. It's about exhibiting grace, dignity and civility, which creates those things around us. If we all went through our days with a *bella figura*, isn't that an environment where we'd all want to be?

Even though the previous part of this chapter addressed our appearance, the goal here isn't about being the best looking person in your circle. That's because exterior beauty with a shallow soul is only decoration. Being attractive goes much deeper than just the cut of a suit or a perfect figure. It's also not about your income. No matter what our bank balance is, we can still live out this key Italian trait.

The following are some of the components of *la bella figura*. I'd encourage you to spend time with people born and raised in Italy or older Italian-Americans to pick up the subtleties of this art of living.

• Don't say, "Ciao!" (How to not be a *"mammaluke"* ["idiot"])

Many years ago, I was in a café owned by a man from Milan. We were having a conversation when an older Italian couple joined us. When I had to leave, I said "Ciao!" to everyone. As I went out the door, I heard the woman say to the café owner, "Did she just say 'ciao' to us?" She was offended, and rightfully so.

Whether we're in the Old World or New, it's polite to speak to others with a respectful tone rather than a casual one. This is especially true when we address someone older than us or an authority figure.

Use a person's title and last name until he or she encourages a more informal interaction. For example, continue to say "Dr. Iacono" or "Mrs. Petrucci" until they suggest you use their first names.

Of course, if you're talking to a younger person or a peer, it's appropriate to be more casual.

As a note, Italians love titles! Anyone who's graduated from college is often addressed as "Doctor." So, when you're in the *Bel Paese*, don't expect medical advice from your new friend Dottoressa Galano because she may have a degree in literature or political science. However, she'll probably share her recipe for *pastina* which is the cure-all for any health woes!

• Be on time, and have a steak…depending where you are!

As a former engineer, I like precision. As someone who has wasted a lot of time during my life, I am acutely aware of its value. I believe that punctuality is polite, and it shows that I'm not more important than others.

Promptness has a cultural interpretation. If you've ever traveled to Italy, you know this is true. My father experienced this when he was a plant manager in Mexico: "tomorrow" meant a time in the future, not necessarily the day after today.

So, to demonstrate a *bella figura* when traveling, conform to the customs there. We're guests in their country. It would be a *brutta figura* (bad impression) to expect them to abide by our beliefs. For example, some cultures think we're sacrilegious by eating beef. So, don't ask for a t-bone if you're in India.

The bottom line is the old adage about when we're in Rome, to do as the Romans do. Of course, if something is immoral, unethical or illegal, you can choose not to participate. Just be open to the thought that your way might not be the only way.

Here are some additional *bella figura* ways to show respect:

- Open doors for others and especially for your elders.

- Take off your hat when going inside and when the National Anthem playing.

- Bring a small gift, like flowers or chocolates, when invited to someone's home for a meal. (Don't bring chrysanthemums since they are used for funeral arrangements!)

- Take the time to ask about a person's life before talking about yourself. This is true in business meetings, too.

- Do not assume that every Italian has a family member in The Mob. Otherwise, I have a cousin who will break your legs! Just kidding!!

- Avoid making jokes about the Pope, the Mafia, or Italy's role in World War II. As in the bullet point above this one, we can make fun of ourselves; it's bad form for someone else to do so.

I encourage you to embrace both the literal and figurative meanings of *la bella figura*. You and I can drop a pebble in the pond of politeness, and the ripple effects might change the world—eventually!

*Courtesy is not superficial. Let's say that it's a combination of intuition, professionalism and humanity...
taking care of your neighbor as yourself.*

—Beppe Severgnini

CHAPTER 10
VOLARE (TO FLY)

WHAT MAKES YOUR HEART SOAR?

How would you like to be healthier, more productive, and have deeper relationships? Since you're reading this book, I'll bet that you enthusiastically said, "Yes!" You can have all that and more by—drum roll, please—being happy.

Okay, how many of you just sighed with disappointment? Stick with me here to learn about the actual science behind this key element to a fulfilling life. No matter what your circumstances, you can choose to find joy. A positive outlook will help you navigate through the storms of life.

Further, happiness is a trait that you can learn. So, even if you've been a Grumpy Guido up to now, you can change. Especially when you understand how this can improve your life and the lives of those around you, taking action is the next logical step. Instead of just surviving, you can flourish and help others do the same.

Scientific research shows that happy people:

- have more successful marriages, friendships, and careers.

- get sick less often and recover faster when they are ill.

- donate more to charity (Being benevolent makes you cheerful, too—win-win!).

- are more helpful and more likely to volunteer.

- have an easier time handling tragedies and hardships since optimism lessens grief.

- engage in deeper and more meaningful conversations.

- are more creative problem-solvers and more productive on the job.

- tend to exercise more often and eat in a healthy manner.

- are content rather than being jealous of others.

- live longer than those who are not as happy.[1]

Before we explore how to increase your joy, let's debunk some merriment myths. It's not about your income or where you were born. It also doesn't mean we have to be on cloud nine all the time, nor do we ignore the difficulties around us. Instead, it's vital to look for the good despite the challenges that we face.

Happiness is not an destination; it is something we can experience every day. Don't think that joy will appear after you get that promotion, lose your muffin top, or meet the perfect mate. Finding pleasure even in the mundane is an art that you can eventually master.

Think about the Neapolitan classic song *O Sole Mio*. The writer, Giovanni Capurra, paints a romantic picture of ordinary, everyday things like the air after a storm, or a woman singing while hanging out the laundry. Not exactly the backdrop for a hip-hop music video, but pleasant images that carry our thoughts to a welcoming and beautiful place.

Several years ago, I bought my grandparents' 103-year-old house, and we're still in the process of refurbishing it. Whenever I scrub my hands with Lava soap at the kitchen sink, I'm immediately taken back in time. I picture Uncle Johnny, standing in that very spot,washing his hands each evening when he returned home from work. The simple act of lathering up makes me smile.

I encourage you to look for glimmers of happiness in your daily routine. It could be as common as hearing a favorite song or as awe-inspiring as a spectacular sunset. I'm sure that you can understand the impact of multiplying day-to-day happiness: you're making a bouquet of beautiful thoughts. Although it won't prevent hardships or sadness from entering our lives, it'll help us persevere through them. Just as sending a card to an ill friend doesn't instantly cure the disease, but it'll bring about a smile or two.

Now that you're convinced to pursue happiness, I'll tell you that it's not something to chase! It's a by-product of living out all the principles in this book. Knowing something and putting it into action is what creates the environment for your bliss.

Let's explore some ways to increase your smiles per day!

• Spend time with uplifting friends and family

Did you notice I didn't say to be with just any ol' person? We all know negative Ninos. They're like human vacuum cleaners, sucking all the joy out of every place they go. Yes, there are circumstances where they can't be avoided, such as work and family gatherings. Do your best to tolerate them, and be sure to plan a time to meet up with people who'll jump-start your attitude.

Is your list of friends and family shorter than you'd like? I'd suggest that you re-read chapters six and seven.

• Count your blessings—out loud!

Have you ever tried to express gratitude and think of your problems at the same time? You can't! When we give thanks for all the good in our lives, our minds take a break from all the struggles.

Better than just mentally mulling over these miracles, tell people about them! Call or write to your loved ones. Send a quick text to your friend that always makes you laugh. Dial the phone number of your cousin who helped you through a rough time.

You'll you remind yourself how lucky you are, it'll help them to feel loved and appreciated.

At the very least, review what you're thankful for every day. One study evaluated participants who wrote down those blessings for six weeks.[1] They slept better, felt happier, made healthier food choices, and exercised more. That's a fantastic return on a minimal investment!

• Do unto others

Whether it's volunteering with your favorite non-profit or shoveling the snow from your neighbor's walkway, helping other people is a sure way to lift your spirits.

There are so many worthy causes that'd put your time and money to good use. Find one (or more) that makes your heart melt with either compassion or pride. If you can't volunteer in person, make a monetary donation and promote them on social media.

One note about giving, though: if you're being generous to receive praise or to get something in return, you can forget about the bluebird of happiness landing on your shoulder. It might plop something else there if that's your motivation! Be sure to do your helpful act just because it's the right thing to do.

An excellent example of giving from the heart is the southern Italian practice of *caffè sospeso*. This is when a person pays for an extra coffee to be given to someone in the future that can't afford it. A restaurant in Florence started doing this with pizzas. During the 2020 lockdown, Neapolitans revived a custom with non-perishable food items placed in baskets along the sidewalks. As the father of this movement, Giuseppe Moscati, wrote a century ago, the present-day signs also read, "Those who can, put something in; those who can't, help yourself."

• Do what you love

If money and time weren't concerns, what would you do right now or next month? What were some things you did in the past that brought you joy? What are some activities where you lose track of time?

Whether you enjoy reading or sky-diving, jigsaw puzzles or motorcycles, plan it into your schedule, and don't feel guilty! When you pursue your passions, you are revitalized. That energy will spill over to your entire life, both at home and on the job.

One of my hot buttons is traveling. My overall attitude is cheerful if I have at least one trip on the horizon. Doing research for a place, finding unusual things to do, and figuring out the logistics all invigorate me. I put together a notebook with maps, train schedules, and restaurants to try. I get fired up when planning our next adventure! I know this exhausts some of you. The point is to do the things that ignite a spark in you.

Granted, there are some activities that we cannot do any longer due to physical limitations, family commitments, and other situations. For example, I loved, loved, loved being in theatrical productions. It was magical to combine a myriad of talents to create something where people's hearts could be touched. At this point in my life, I have other priorities. If I truly wanted to pursue this, I'd find a way. Therefore, I consider my theater days as beautiful—not sad—memories, and that's okay.

• Try something new

One of my tenets of life is this: When was the last time you did something for the first time? If I can't remember, it's been too long!

It doesn't have to be over-the-top like bungee jumping. Even just trying a new restaurant or taking a different route to work can be a breath of fresh air in a stagnant life. Novelty can help your brain by keeping it working. It can also bring other points of view to your attention.

What are some of the things that you've always wanted to do? Perhaps your heart skips a beat when you think about driving a race car or taking scuba lessons. Maybe you dream of having high tea in London or a fresh-from-the-oven pizza in Naples.

How about learning a language or a musical instrument? The possibilities are endless and exciting.

My challenge is for you to start investigating how to make it happen. If you want to climb to the top of the *Duomo* in Florence, check out flights and hotels. Ask people who have been there for ideas. Instead of saying *if* you go, tell yourself and others about *when* you will go. More about this make-it-happen technique will be addressed in chapter eleven.

Going on a new adventure with another person doubles—maybe even quadruples—the enjoyment of an event. You'll be able to reminisce and laugh about it for years to come. These shared experiences weave the bonds of relationships into works of art. It also helps you not to back out of something. If your friend is waiting for you at the airport, you're more likely to go sky-diving. Otherwise, it'd be too easy to convince yourself that you're acrophobic.

When is the best time to try something new? As soon as bleepin' possible! We're never guaranteed tomorrow. This became profoundly evident after my first trip to Italy. My life-long dream to go there, with my father and Uncle Johnny, came true in 2001. Fifty weeks later—not 52—my father passed away. If we'd postponed that trip "just one more year," we never would've gone. Not only would I have missed out on some of my most treasured memories, I strongly doubt that I would have the passion for Italy and the phenomenal relationships that I have today.

- Music is a major key (pun intended!) to happiness

I'm not saying that Italians invented music, but they did create the first symphonies, and they introduced notations, like *forte* and *piano*, still used today. While other ethnic groups have written operas, such as Germans and Klingons, the Italians can take credit for the origins of this genre of performance. Related to music, they also wrote the first book about dance and staged the first ballet (from the Italian word *ballare* [to dance]).

Closer to home, my family has a love for music that goes beyond simple enjoyment. Right up there with air, love, and pasta, melodies are necessary to the Matteras. It's like we have a soundtrack to our lives even if it's just in our heads. Most of us with Italian heritage agree.

One of my greatest treasures is the Victrola that my grandfather gave to my grandmother for their first anniversary. Hearing Caruso' voice or a song about no bananas takes me back to my grandparents' living room and the feeling of love that filled the house. Whenever I hear "Walkin' on Sunshine" by Katrina and The Waves, I'm transported back to when I lived in Florence, Italy. Every morning, when I walked by an internet café, they played that song. There's an association with hearing that tune and feeling adventurous and fully alive, as I did in the Renaissance city.

It's not only about pleasant memories. You probably have some favorite songs that lift your spirits and—if no one is looking—make you dance. Make a playlist of tunes that inspire you. It doesn't matter what type of music; it's only important that it makes you sit a little taller, walk a little faster, and smile a little bigger.

Whenever you're preparing for a big presentation or getting ready to tackle the yard work, blast your inspiring playlist. You might want to wear headphones if you're in your office.

A study published in *The Journal of Positive Psychology* showed that people could improve their moods by listening to upbeat music.[2] A Finnish study reported that students who took music classes were happier at school in general.[3]

Likewise, it's wise to have musical selections for every occasion: a romantic dinner at home, backyard barbeque with friends, and I'm-amazed-I-didn't-hit-anyone-at-work evenings. Unless you're gazing at the stars on a grassy hill, hearing crickets can be awkward at social events. Music adds a richer background to any activity.

- Bittersweet: memories

Depending on what's happening in our lives, memories can either be comforting or crushing. On days when all is well, photos of my loved ones who have passed bring smiles to my face. However, near the holidays, those same pictures poke at the wound that hasn't yet healed in my heart.

When you think back on the wonderful events that have happened and the precious souls in your life, I hope you are happy more than you are sad. If you do weep for the loss of days gone by, that only shows the depth of your emotions. Don't be embarrassed; the world needs more authentic and caring people.

If you find yourself on a downward spiral when thinking about the past, I'd suggest reframing your perspective. Yes, those days are history and those people are gone; we can never recreate those times. Yet, those very same memories are proof that there is joy in life. You had it once, you can find it again. That brings us hope and can revive our souls!

From a tough-love perspective, we always have a choice. We can choose to wallow in self-pity or we can decide to live with joy. Of course, we need to take time to process our pain, but don't stay there too long. I'd guess that your loved ones in Heaven would want you to move forward.

As far as a vastly different society now vs. the past, I agree. It seems that only a minority of us have manners, let alone respect and patriotism. Yet, choosing to be down-trodden does not help at all. We continue to do the best we can in our corners of the world. Decide to be the one that keeps the torch lit because it only takes a small candle to chase away the darkness. Be the light!

- Find Meaning

No, I'm not going to tell you to find your passion. Many people are frustrated when given that assignment because they think that means curing cancer or performing some other incredible feat. Instead, let's identify this down-to-earth, readily achievable component of happiness.

A meaningful life is when you feel connected to a greater purpose. That's it! For one person, it means a career; for another, it's all about spirituality. Parents and grandparents often say how their lives are fulfilled because of their families—and they have the photos in their wallets and phones to prove it!

A word of caution: don't judge what someone else defines as meaningful. My father was a workaholic, gone from 6 a.m. to 6 p.m. or later during the week. In his free time, he read books to help him be a better manager. The man had no hobbies, and everyone was on a mission to find him one. However, he simply loved his career. Not only was he proud to contribute to the company's success but he also looked at his position as a way to help entire families.

After my father's funeral in his home town of Providence, RI, there was a memorial service in Tijuana, Mexico, where he was a manufacturing facility manager for over a decade. (They lived in San Diego.) For hours, family after family expressed their thanks, love, and appreciation for all that "Mr. Joe" had done for them. They told stories of how my father, out of his own pocket, gave his workers food, medicine, paper goods, and mostly, respectful compassion. During the summers, he would host picnics for his employees and their families. He loved seeing everyone laughing and enjoying the day.

No matter how you spend your time, look for how you can be a part of something beyond yourself. Even at a job you dread, you can positively affect those around you. Get more involved with your church or a civic group. Sign up for a walk-a-thon or offer to teach a class at the library.

The search for significance isn't found by ascending a mountain to seek out a wise man. Like a hidden gem, it's right there, already in your life, waiting to be discovered and to shine.

Somebody should tell us, right at the start of our lives,
that we are dying. Then, we might live life to the limit,
every minute of every day. Do it! Whatever you want,
do it now! There are only so many tomorrows.

—Pope Paul VI

CHAPTER 11
IMPARO ANCORA.
(I'M STILL LEARNING.)
—MICHELANGELO, AGE 87

I'M TOO OLD AND OTHER ASSORTED EXCUSES

During one of my solo trips to Italy, my dear friend Frank Romano (mentioned in chapter one) was visiting his family near Naples. We planned to meet at the main train station and then enjoy a coffee and conversation.

I arrived early and stood near the taxi stand, which was our meeting point. A dashing Italian approached me, and we chatted a bit. He invited me for *qualcosa da bere* (a drink), but I explained that I was waiting for a friend. He then said that he'd wait, in case my friend didn't come. While I was waiting for Frank, two other Italians made the same proposition. (By the way, I was 15 years younger and 20 pounds lighter!) The three Romeos were hovering.

Finally, Frank arrived! We embraced and walked arm-in-arm to a nearby café. The wanna-be Latin lovers were shocked because my date was a man in his *eighties*. I'm not sure if they were discouraged or inspired.

Whether it's a Renaissance master or a retired Army colonel, the Italian spirit soars when looking at life as something to embrace and not just something to endure. Age isn't a factor. I look at Frank, who has lived almost a century, and is still independent. Just a few years ago, he started day trading; he's having fun taking on Wall Street.

My grandparents continued to do the things they loved for as long as they could. Grandpa kept making wine, and Grandma continued to host Sunday dinners. Uncle Johnny was a voracious reader and kept up with current events. He could talk to anybody about any topic. He shared his discoveries with others by giving them articles he'd clipped out of the newspaper that he thought they'd enjoy.

Just because the number of candles on the birthday cake could set off a fire alarm, there's no reason to stop living with a sense of purpose. No matter how long the future will last for us, we can still contribute to it and enjoy it.

Maybe you wish that you finished that degree or learned to play the piano. You sadly move that under the too old category of your hopes & dreams list. You may say something like, "Why bother? I'd be 50 when I graduate." Guess what! You're going to be 50 anyway; why not achieve something that will enrich your life?

Perhaps your age isn't what's holding you back. You might think that you're stuck because of the economy, bigotry, or some other outside factor. I won't list the myriad of examples of how people with your same obstacles overcame them. You can easily research that for yourself.

All the excuses that we blame for our ordinary and dull selves point back to an underlying thought: we don't believe that we can achieve those dreams. We doubt that we can make a difference in our own lives, let alone the world.

My father sparked my interest in how our thoughts affect our lives. Although he never finished high school, he became a general manager with an international company. He introduced me to authors like Dale Carnegie and Zig Ziglar. My father was my mentor as I climbed the corporate ladder. Whether we were six or thirty-six, he always told us that we could do anything.

Before we proceed, please know that I'm not talking about just robotically repeating positive self-talk mantras. Yes, it's important to replace the discouraging automated thoughts in our heads with encouraging truths. However, those seeds won't grow if the conditions aren't right.

This is also not about a name-it-and-claim-it approach because God is not a vending machine. Plus, what happens if I keep saying that I'm skinny or that I'll have that Lamborghini, but I don't believe it in my heart? I will subconsciously feel that I'm lying. So, I force myself to keep saying the right things which only makes it worse. It's like putting another coat of paint over a rust spot. Sure, it's okay for a while, but the root of the problem will eventually reappear.

For some of us, it's not so much the belief in our abilities. Instead, we question if we are enough. If you know exactly what I mean by that, you're not alone. For the readers who don't understand, let me explain.

Imagine an actor, but not a famous one. Even though he has performed all over the world and has a few gold statues on his bookshelf, he's constantly auditioning for the next role. Time after time, he's told that he's not tall enough, young enough, or ethnic enough. Never enough. Maybe you've experienced this in your career.

In my case, there were life events that hardwired these feelings. As one example, I'm the only one of my siblings born out of wed-lock. My parents got married when my mother was pregnant with my sister; I was ten. That was among the first programming of this destructive code into my mind. In this case, I wasn't enough for them to get married. I remember a boy telling me that my weight is why he wouldn't date me. I wasn't thin enough. Decades later, my then-husband brought over divorce papers after 20+ years of wedded blah. (No, that's not a typo!) He said that he never loved me romantically. Ouch! More code added to my brain's software: not enough to be in a long-term love relationship.

I won't bore you with the exhausting and depressing list of occurrences during my life that reinforced this mindset. I will, however, share how I'm overcoming this lie. Right there is the first step: recognize that it isn't the truth!

For one thing, anything that is rare is valuable. Just like the Mona Lisa or the Hope Diamond, there's only one you. Even if you're an identical twin, you are 100% original. Your fingerprint is the one-of-a-kind factory seal!

Most of us started down that rocky road of not feeling enough because of other people's opinions. While I'm certainly not defending anyone who deeply hurt you, I do ask you to consider why. More than likely, they took out their insecurities on you because they were also made to feel worthless by someone else. Again, I'm not condoning their behavior; we just might not know the whole story.

Granted, some sadistic jerks take pleasure in making people feel inferior. Maybe it was someone you admired or even loved. If that's the case, please recognize that *they* weren't good enough for *you,* not vice versa. Those kinds of people would use *The David* as a coat rack or paint over *The Last Supper*. You don't need that in your life.

I also encourage you to think about times when you were enough. Perhaps you stood by someone's side when they went through a dark time in their life. Maybe you got that promotion or diploma. Don't dismiss those moments when you were the knight in shining armor or the winner on the platform.

To further prove that you're enough, I'd like you to think about someone you love beyond measure. Even though that person is imperfect, you love them anyway. They are enough for you, right? Therefore, the same can be said about you. I'm positive that there are people who love you, flaws and all. You're enough for the people who matter.

I'd be remiss if I didn't bring up two perspectives that may sting regarding this topic. If you want to have an authentic, ful- filled and meaningful life, sometimes we need to hear counsel that hurts but will help us. Know that I'm saying this in a spirit of love.

First, we just looked at how the people you care about are enough. However, are they enough in *all* areas? For instance, there are people that I'd trust with my life, but not with editing this book for grammar. There are people who I can depend on without question, but I wouldn't ask them for advice on investments.

They are enough for me, but not enough for every part of my existence. So, why do we expect to be 100% enough for someone else? Not only is that unrealistic, but it also puts too much responsibility on that one person. Actually, it's selfish to think that way.

The second unpleasant viewpoint is, "So what?" Let's pretend that you're *not* enough. So the flip what? We can have a big pity party or we can go out there and do our best anyway. Isn't that actually liberating? It's your life! Pursue your dreams! Your adventure will be so amazing that you won't have time to worry if you're enough for anyone or not.

HOPE IS THE SEED OF BELIEF!

Having said all that, you may still have doubts. Maybe you just can't believe in yourself, but I'll bet you at least have hope. That's great news! Why? Because hope is the seed of belief! All the tragedies in your life haven't buried you. Rather, you've been planted!

Let's look at practical steps to help that seed grow into full-fledged belief. No heavenly vending machine required.

1) Question the stories you tell yourself.

- Do they help or hurt you? Are they even true?

- Start telling yourself about who you want to become.

- Saying, "I'm the greatest piano player in the world!" might feel phony. Instead, here are some truthful and inspiring ways to tell your new story:

  - "I will be (or, am becoming) ____." For example, I am becoming a talented piano player.

- Add the word "yet" to a current perception. For example, I don't know how to play the piano yet.

2) Associate with people who have what you want.

- Join civic and online groups that have members that you admire.

- World-renowned teachers can mentor you by reading their books or listening to their podcasts.

3) Act as if you already are the person you want to become.

- How does your future successful self act, think, and treat others? It costs nothing to have good posture, to respond versus react, or to be polite.

- What will you be wearing and driving? I'm not saying to spend money you don't have. However, you can start to dress the part with what you own now. You can take care of your current vehicle like you would if it was a Ferrari. You wouldn't leave empty coffee cups in the floorboards of your F8 Tributo, would you?

4) What would your best friend or grandmother say about you?

- We're often our worst critic. The people who love you the most probably believe in your abilities more than you do.

- If we were to interview your best friend, what would be at least two strengths we'd hear about you? What would Grandma or Grandpa say?

  - If you're not sure of the responses, ask them! If your grandparents are in Heaven with mine, think of times when you *knew* and *felt* their love.

You've probably heard the quote about being careful with your thoughts because they become your words, which become your actions, and, eventually, your destiny. It's true because our brains work to prove whatever we believe. Thankfully, we can learn to change that.

As my father often said, it's not so much about what happens, but how we think about it will ultimately determine the result. Here's the pattern:

Fact → Thought → Emotion → Action → Outcome

For example, Anna is discouraged and scared because she's been out of work for months. She imagines that everything would be better if she'd only find a job. Here's her current thinking:

Fact: Anna is out of work
Thought: Anna feels like a loser
Emotion: She feels defeated and hopeless
Action: Anna half-heartedly looks for a job, but ends up watching cat videos
Outcome: She doesn't get any interviews

Do you see what happens here? Anna's actions determine the outcome, which ultimately confirms what she believes, and the depressing cycle continues.

As a note, we often confuse the thoughts and emotions as being facts. They're not; they're opinions. Another person may also be unemployed (fact), but he doesn't call himself hateful names (opinion).

To improve the self-fulfilling prophecy, we need to change our thoughts. Let's consider a new way to look at this.

Fact: Anna is out of work
Thought: This is an opportunity to find a better job or start a business

Emotion: She is encouraged—maybe even excited—about the future
Action: Anna updates her resume' and starts to network with others
Outcome: She applies for more jobs which increases her chances for interviews

Once we change our thoughts, we next need to do something, anything! Even the smallest step in the right direction makes a difference. You'll succeed at that, and gain the confidence to take another step.

I know that reprogramming our automatic thoughts can be daunting. Following are some of the most common destructive ideas, and how we can replace them with realistic and productive ones.

As you review these, remember that they are most likely to occur when you're tired, overwhelmed, stressed and/or ill. So, be sure to get enough sleep, ask for help, relax when you can, and stay healthy.

• (Mis)fortune Telling: Predicting the worst outcome

No one's life is perfect, but neither is it an all-out disaster. Sometimes, we jump to a doomed conclusion when facing uncertain situations. For example, we might say, "If I don't lose weight, I'll never find love." Or we may think, "*The pain in my leg won't go away. Do I have cancer?*"

When these anxiety-causing thoughts creep into your mind, capture them immediately! They're not facts; they're merely potential outcomes. That means that other and less terrifying results are also possible.

If your best friend verbalized those dire predictions, what would you say? You'd remind them that most things we worry about never happen. You would also encourage them to have a plan for that worst-case scenario, and to consider more positive conclusions.

- Fake ID: Labeling yourself with your mistakes

As humans, we're masters of missteps and can blunder like a boss. The problem arises when we wear those failures like a scarlet letter tattooed to our foreheads. Maybe you tripped while walking down the aisle, and now you describe yourself as a klutz. Perhaps you were in a series of failed romantic relationships, so you identify as unlovable or even promiscuous.

When we label ourselves, we impose limits on our growth and opportunities for the future. That's because we never rise above how we picture ourselves. I'll share a friend's story of how this happens.

Silvia and her sister are identical twins. However, their personalities are polar opposites. Silvia is a high-energy extrovert with a flair for the dramatic. Her sibling is soft-spoken and studious.

When the girls were growing up, family and neighbors often remarked about the differences. They would say things like, "When they're teenagers, Silvia is going to be trouble!" What do you think she became? You got it: trouble! She spent more time in the principal's office than in class, and she hung around with the wrong crowd. She became the identity that others assigned to her.

The good news is that Silvia did turn her life around. She eventually removed that limiting label and created new empowering ones. That means you can, too. It doesn't matter if other people gave you these dubious titles or if they are self-imposed.

It's important to recognize that the past doesn't equal the future. Just because you failed yesterday, you're not always going to fail tomorrow. Therefore, stop calling yourself by these names that are holding you back.

Next, take inventory of your skills, talents, and successes. Then, remind yourself of them every day. These are the accurate and true definitions of your identity. You decide what kind of person you want to be, and you will become exactly that.

- Should-a/could-a/would-a: Reliving the past with judgment

Related to the labels from the past that we wear like nametags, we tend to berate ourselves for making poor choices. We lose sleep as we relive the event in our heads. We think about the snappy come-backs that we could've said or the better decision we should've made.

The simplest—but not necessarily easiest—thing to do is learn from it and move forward. We cannot go back in time, so why let our focus stay there? Like Enzo Ferrari said, "What's behind you doesn't matter."

Perhaps you're discouraged because you haven't reached a particular goal, and you think that you should have by now. You start to doubt that you ever will. Maybe even other people are telling you to stop daydreaming. However, if you truly want something, ignore the naysayers.

Until 1954, everyone believed that the human body would collapse when trying to run a mile in less than four minutes. Well, not everyone. Roger Bannister was the first person to break not only the record but also the belief. Less than two months later, another runner was even faster. Since then, hundreds have achieved the once impossible goal.

Was there some technological breakthrough with shoes in 1954? Did gravity change? No. The difference was belief. If one person did it, so can another. Your four-minute mile is the life you dream about becoming a reality. It starts with the idea that it's possible.

As you increase your belief, your confidence grows. This doesn't happen overnight; it comes from practice, which means the daily reprogramming of your mind. Think about when you first learned to drive. With a white-knuckle grip on the wheel, you looked both ways thirteen times before turning into the street. Now, however, it's second nature because you've driven many, many miles.

Practice doesn't make perfect, but it does make improvements. Keep doing what needs to be done while hoping and believing! Heck, if cauliflower can become pizza, you can surely do anything!

One last belief builder I'd like to address is faith. I'm not talking about going to church or reading a Bible. I'm talking about faith in something bigger than us that wants the best for us. You may call it a Higher Power or The Universe while I call it God.

My father passed away on May 11, 2002. After going home to Colorado after the funeral, I found a bougainvillea blossom on my front step. While those plants flourished at my parents' house in southern California, they were rare in the Rocky Mountains. Further, if there were any bougainvilleas in my area, they wouldn't be in bloom in the middle of May.

A month later, I was in the home improvement section of a megastore. I picked up a three-way socket and saw "Leviton Mexico" printed on it. That was the facility that my father managed. I burst into tears, thinking that he might have held this very socket. I'm sure the other customer in the aisle wasn't sure why electrical supplies were so emotional.

I interpret the flower on my stairs and the Mexican socket as two of many messages from God that show His care and concern. My faith teaches that God loves us. You and I want only the best for those we love. So, can you imagine how much more a perfect God desires that for us? You may struggle with a belief in yourself, but trust me that God sees your bright future. It's now up to you to pursue it!

Count your nights by stars, not shadows;
count your life with smiles, not tears.

—Italian proverb

CHAPTER 12
AVANTI! (GO FORTH!)

PASTA & MAGIC

D id you know that you could eat a different pasta shape every night for a year before repeating one? Now, that's a challenge I'd gladly accept! Yes, Italians eat a lot of pasta: 40 or more pounds a year, and that's per person.

From a culinary perspective, different shapes of pasta are more suited to certain types of sauces. The Pasta Police won't arrest you for putting Bolognese on your *bucatini*, but there are better choices that take a dish from good to great. Likewise, you can do an acceptable job with pretty much any task, but there are others where you'll excel. That's where you go from ordinary to extraordinary, from indifference to intensity. That's using your noodle!

Yes, there are things we must do that don't spark joy. For example, those clothes aren't going to fold themselves. We also do things that pass the time but don't improve the quality of our lives. This is where the Pareto Principle comes to the table.

The Italian economist Vilfredo Pareto noticed that 80% of the land in Italy was owned by 20% of the people. He noticed that this 80/20 principle was also true in other parts of our lives. As a note, it's not always that exact ratio; it could be 90/10. The point is that the minority of actions produces the majority of results. Here are some other examples:

- We wear 20% of our clothing 80% of the time

- Ten percent of our friends bring us 90% of our meaningful connections

- Only 15 to 20% of parishioners fund most of a church's budget

Let's look at how to leverage the Pareto Principle to have a fulfilling life that inspires those around you. Federico Fellini said, "Life is a combination of magic and pasta." This is where the magic happens. You don't even need a wizard's hat or wand.

Make a list of ten things you need to do today. What are two items on that list that will most impact where you want to be or what you want to achieve? For example, for someone who wants to publish a book, writing 500 words could be a must-do for today. If someone wants to strengthen family relationships, spending an hour together after dinner might be at the top of the list. Simple enough, so far, right?

However, have you noticed that we often spend most of our time on the other eight things? It could be because the 80% is usually easier and faster to do. That 20% might seem overwhelming, or there may even be some fear involved. So, we work on the simpler eight tasks.

When we do this, day after day, it's obvious why we still haven't achieved our dreams by the time we thought we would have. We've been busy but not necessarily productive.

You see, most of us learned about time management. But what we really need to learn is priority management. No one wants to reach their golden years with regrets. We can avoid that heartbreak by having a crystal-clear vision of what's most important and what you want to achieve. Always remember the legacy you want to build.

Pareto and the Priorities (No, it's not a new band!)

You've already read about the highest Italian priorities in this book: family, friends and faith. I'm sure that other ethnic groups share the same ideals. When making decisions, we learned to consider how it would affect those three pillars of our lives. But we don't always make the best choices! When we realize the errors of our ways, it's usually because we neglected the core values that are nearest and dearest to our hearts.

Step One: Establish your priorities. You saw that coming! Aside from the big three just mentioned, you may have other passions like the environment, animals or world hunger. Whatever makes your heart swell with love and compassion is your priority.

Step Two: Set goals that line up with what you decided in Step One. There will definitely be personal objectives, but don't forget ones that include your family or favorite organizations. What would success mean to you in your career? How would you describe the ideal relationship with your partner? What could your church or civic group do to further help its members and neighbors in your community?

Frank DiPiero, Chicago businessman and host of the *Keepin' It Real* podcast, has a brilliant idea that weaves together your goals and keeping the spirit of your heritage alive. He calls it the Italian Bucket List; of course, you might have a Greek, Muscle Car, or Gelato Bucket List. According to Frank, the first entry should be "Go to Italy!" Can you see how your unique list can be an exciting way to take your life from mediocre to remarkable? Have fun with this!

Step Three: What can you do today to reach those goals? What can you do this week or month? Breaking down that top-of-the-mountain, ultimate goal into smaller, more believable steps, you're more likely to achieve it.

Schedule these actions in your calendar instead of only having a to-do list. If you randomly wrote "dentist" on a notepad, you'd probably never get your teeth cleaned until it was a desperate situation. However, if it's right there on your calendar, on Tuesday at noon, you'll go.

By putting these items on your calendar, you'll probably actually do them. You also see why you're always overwhelmed and constantly carrying them over to the next week…and the next. It helps you to identify what's truly important, and how you might be wasting time.

<u>Pareto Principle Point:</u> Do something every day towards your goals *before* letting all the little distractions eat up your time. The important tasks are the ones that only you can do or the ones that you love to do. Try to address them when you're at your peak of energy, whether you're an early bird or a night owl like me. (My parents should have named me Dusk!)

I'm sure you've heard motivational speakers tell you just to *decide* to change your life. I've even said that, but I didn't explain the history behind the word. In Italian and Latin, the verb is *decidere* which means "to cut off." You see, when you decide to do something, you're cutting off other options. For example, when you decide to marry someone, you no longer have other romantic relationships—unless you're looking for trouble! After all, a love triangle eventually becomes a wreck-tangle. (Oh, c'mon! You're going to use that one!)

Likewise, once you decide to go after your goals, you agree to cut off anything that distracts you from that mission. Sometimes, we let go of activities like spending hours watching TV to attend classes or go for walks with our loved ones. It could be as simple but profound as deciding who you'll never let yourself be again. Starting today, you are a new person; the old you is gone.

It's been said that Michelangelo carved The David by chipping away at the marble that trapped him. You can chip away at the clutter that traps your dreams. Decide what kind of life you want. Then, when possible, cut off everything else.

SHHH! A LITTLE SECRET TO BIG SUCCESS

If I could tell you an inside scoop about how to increase your chances of success by 40%, would you want to know? Of course, you would! Okay, here it is: (whispering) write it down!

I know you were hoping for some mystical incantation or a long-lost DaVinci code. However, the simple act of writing down what you want can radically improve your outcome. For one thing, only about 20% of the population puts pen to paper about their goals. (There's the Pareto Principle at work again!)

Why does this seemingly insignificant act of writing something down have such an impact? First of all, think about the times that have you gone to the store for just a few items, and one was a must-buy. We don't write a list because it's only a handful of groceries; we don't even need a cart. How many of those times did you forget that one important item? That's because there's so much bombarding our minds at all times.

Having that grocery list or your goals on paper keeps it in the forefront of your mind. Like a pop-up on your computer, it's easy for your brain to access and to remember.

Writing down your goals also kicks in what neuropsychologists call the "generation effect." No, it's not about baby boomers or millennials. The act of generating something vastly improves our focus and recall of it compared to only reading about it or watching it.

There's another phenomenon happening: memory encoding. Basically, the hippocampus in your brain analyzes the flood of input and decides what to keep and discard. If it's significant information, it gets stored in your long-term memory.

It's actually a process of synapses and neurotransmitters, energy, and chemicals. Like practicing a speech or a dance routine, you're encoding your goals into your long-term memory. Your brain then accepts that as a fact that will, of course, happen. We could say it's a no-brainer!

Here's a bonus little secret to big success: find an accountability partner. This person doesn't need to be an expert in your field or even give you advice. It's simply someone who'll commit to holding you accountable.

When I started to write this book, I asked three friends of mine to fill this role for me. They had my permission to ask me, at any time, about my progress. Just knowing that they could pop the question today or tomorrow, helped keep me on track. It was a matter of personal pride.

In addition to a person holding you accountable, just making a public declaration of your intention works wonders. For example, I recently did a presentation for an international Italian group. During the Q&A, one of the hosts asked when my next book would be published. Not only did the members on the live webinar know the date, anyone listening to the recording in the future would be able to see if I kept my word!

So, do yourself a favor: write down what you want your ideal life to look like, and find someone to hold you accountable. Don't forget the power of announcing your goals to the world. It may be just the push that you need.

GOING FROM NOW TO WOW!

I won't take up space here to address how to identify the most worthwhile goals for you. That's because numerous resources teach this. Plus, you probably already know how. If not, just remember that goals should be SMART: Specific, Measurable, Achievable, Realistic, and Time-sensitive.

As we strive toward the new and improved version of ourselves, we sometimes just get tired of struggling. I can relate. However, you want to be fulfilled, happy, and inspiring, right? That means getting to the other side of the pond. Let me explain.

When we start making changes to move forward, we're pretty clear about what we *don't* want. We don't want to be financially strapped. We don't want to see a higher number on the scale. We don't want to argue—again—with our spouse.

That's like getting into a boat on one side of a pond, and someone pushes you off the shore. You're drifting along, and it's going well. Yet, we become stuck in the middle of the pond. Why? Because the pain of what we *didn't* want is no longer there; it's not powerful enough to propel us the rest of the way.

For example, Silvia wants to lose 40 pounds. She didn't want to go up another size in clothing, and she didn't want to need insulin. She begins to lose weight but plateaus around the half-way mark. That's because she went down a size or two, and she's no longer pre-diabetic. Of course, she feels better, and people praise her success, but she isn't where she wants to be.

So, how does Silvia reach her goal weight? How do you and I avoid settling for less than what we truly want? We do that by knowing *why* we want to get to the other side of the pond. That gives us oars! It's more powerful and effective to strive toward something we truly want than it is to run away from something undesirable.

WILLPOWER FADES.
WHY POWER PROPELS.

When I was young, my father was a chain smoker. Like anyone with a bad habit, he knew *how* to quit. After decades of smoking, a doctor finally gave him the motivation: my mother was pregnant with my sister. The wise physician recognized my father's temperament—and ego! He said to my father, "Joe, you can keep on smoking. Just know that another man will be raising your new baby because you'll be dead." My father never picked up another cigarette again.

Next to the items on your list of written-down goals, add details of your motivation to achieve them. Some of your entries will be tangible rewards like a weekend getaway or a jacket that caught your eye. For the more philanthropic goals, the reasons may be improving the lives of veterans, keeping family traditions alive, or inspiring young musicians. Once you know the why, the how will figure out itself. That's because your RAS (discussed in chapter five) will work overtime to get what you so dearly want.

Since we're visual creatures, I'd suggest getting pictures of things that you will do or have when you hit certain milestones. A brochure from a tropical resort will inspire you to make those cold calls or stay on the treadmill. Edit a photo to add you and your family to a fireside or beach scene; that cements the vision of a happy future together.

Breaking Though the Blockades

There are a million reasons why we don't push ourselves to do more. Most of them are self-imposed. Many of those obstacles are addressed throughout this book. Another is that we think we've failed too many times. How could anyone learn from a loser?

So, you've tried for the golden ring and missed. You've climbed the ladder only to be knocked down a rung or more. Don't believe the myth that only those who never fail are the winners. In fact, you're more inspiring and relatable when you fall and then rise.

Like Rocky Balboa said in the 2006 movie of the same name, "It ain't about how hard you hit; it's about how hard you can get hit and keep moving forward."

Think about how boring and unrealistic the *Rocky* movies would have been if the Italian Stallion's journey was easy; just one mountaintop experience after another. In the aforementioned film, Rocky also said, "The world ain't all sunshine and rainbows."

Your failures aren't permanent if you learned from them; they're actually lessons. Failure is an event, not a person. When others see your mistakes, they realize theirs don't have to hold them back, either.

Another barrier is telling ourselves that we can't do something. Granted, some physical laws can't be broken, at least in this universe. However, we need to examine our can'ts.

Years ago, my team and I were having a lunch meeting before opening the doors to our class. I complained (whined?) that I didn't have enough time to exercise. I said, "I can't do cardio or weights with my schedule." A kind-hearted colleague asked me, "Can't or won't?"

At first, I was taken aback by the question. However, since I knew she spoke with a spirit of love, I quickly swallowed my pride and offense. She was absolutely right.

I challenge you to write down all the reasons you believe that you can't achieve what you truly want. It might look something like:

I can't start a business.
I can't eat right and exercise.
I can't inspire someone else.

Now, cross out the word "can't" and replace it with "won't." Read the revised sentences. Ouch...especially that last one!

We have a choice: we can make excuses, or we can make a difference. Since you're still reading, I know you want the latter. Go back in this chapter where we discuss having a defined reason why you want to chase after your goals. You won't be held back by can't/won't statements any longer. That's good because the world needs the one and only you!

One way that most of us get distracted from our mission is the internet. We start by doing research or looking for inspiration; there's nothing wrong with that. Before we know it, we spent an hour (or more!) looking at cat videos or taking quizzes to discover what kind of pasta we are!

Make a deal with yourself right now to commit to doing what it takes. As best-selling author and entrepreneur Marie Forleo says, "Create before you consume." If you're an artist or writer, it's easy to see what it means to make something. If you're in a service-based business, you might think that you don't create anything. Not so! You can come up with a new marketing plan or a better way to organize your office. The point is to promise yourself to work toward your priorities before taking a break with frivolous pastimes.

BEGIN AND GOD PROVIDES THE REST –ITALIAN PROVERB

When I returned from my second trip to Italy, I told Uncle Johnny about my adventures as a solo traveler. He happily listened to my tales about figuring out trains, boats, and hotels, and the interesting people I met along the way. What impressed him most, though, was that I crossed the street in Naples by myself. No, really.

If you've ever been to *Napoli*, you know the chaotic energy that surges there. Traffic signals are merely suggestions, and navigating the streets is not for the faint of heart, even in a taxi. Like anyone who has faced a life-or-death situation, Uncle Johnny vividly remembered the scene.

After saying, "You're kiddin' me!" several times, he asked me how I managed to dodge cars and scooters to go across unharmed. I told him that I considered my options and just went!

The opportunities in life are often like that. Whether you want to start a new business or finally take that Bucket List trip, do something. You don't need to know all 37 steps, just the first one or two. Consider your best options and go before your brain talks you out of it.

What about that little voice or twinge of fear that makes you question the idea and, maybe, your sanity? Entrepreneur and author Marie Forleo suggests paying attention to the immediate reaction you have when you think about this grand plan. Does your spirit instantly draw into hiding, or do you have a sudden feeling of expanding?

In other words, trust your intuition. Your survival-focused brain will always tell you to proceed with extra caution. If you're even a little excited about this new venture, and it's legal, ethical, and moral, go for it! If you don't have a sense of peace, perhaps now isn't the time. Just be sure that you're not using that as an excuse to forgo chasing your dreams.

Don't let another day pass without a vision for how you want your life to be and a plan to make it happen! Then, *avanti* (go forth)!

Desire is the key to motivation, but it's determination and commitment to an unrelenting pursuit of your goal—a commitment to excellence—that will enable you to attain the success you seek.

— Mario Andretti

CHAPTER 13
ANDIAMO! (LET'S GO!)

LOVE AND LEGACY

F irst, let's address the numerological elephant in the room. In many cultures, misfortune and mayhem are associated with the number thirteen. However, in Italy, it's actually a lucky number. Life is often like that: it often depends on your perspective.

Likewise, how we interpret our place in the world can depend on our point of view. Some people live from a basis of fear and scarcity. So, they adopt a self-centered mindset, only looking out for themselves. I suspect that you, however, have a different outlook. You and I want to make positive contributions, and we recognize that our actions—good or bad—affect others.

RIPPLES IN A POND

My favorite movie is Frank Capra's *It's a Wonderful Life*. The main character, George Bailey, was frustrated that he didn't accomplish all that he'd dreamed of doing. Like many people, he believed that his life was insignificant.

Miraculously, George had the opportunity to see what would have happened to his loved ones if he'd never been born. In case you've never seen the movie, put this book down and go watch it. No, really. I'll wait.

[Two hours and ten minutes later...] Okay, let's continue!

George came to realize that our actions are like ripples in a pond. For example, if he wasn't there to save his little brother from an icy pond, hundreds of men would've died on an aircraft carrier years later. We may do something that is small in our eyes, but we may never know how that action can affect countless others.

You see, having a meaningful and successful life is not all about us. It's about how many other people we can help along the way. We may not have the biggest bank account or thousands of social media followers. Yet, how we invest in other people's lives is priceless. To paraphrase the toast made my George Bailey's brother, you can be the richest man (or woman) in town!

DON'T FIND YOUR PASSION!

Surprised? Many self-help gurus will tell you to find your passion. What if I told you to find your emotion or feeling? You'd likely be disappointed because you know that emotions and feelings—like passion—fluctuate. They often depend on our mood, energy level and other people's responses.

Instead, I suggest that you find your purpose. Like a soldier in battle, it doesn't matter if you're tired or sad, or what the opposing side does. You have a mission that you're committed to seeing through to fulfillment.

To help define your purpose, consider this quote by Pope Francis:

> *Rivers do not drink their own water;*
> *trees don't eat their own fruit.*
> *Living for others is a rule of nature.*
> *Life is good when you are happy, but much bet-*
> *ter when others are happy because of you.*

In my opinion, our purpose is to contribute to our world, to make it better for our families, friends and communities. My grandparents—and, possibly yours—did that by coming to America and creating a legacy. Out of respect and love, I want to do my part. Even if you don't know the stories of your ancestors, you most likely want to make a difference. You can!

OUR PURPOSE: CONTRIBUTE & COLLABORATE

Now that I've told you not to pursue your passion, you might be scratching your head and wondering how to define your purpose. It's where these three things intersect:

➤ What you're good at doing

➤ What you love to do

➤ What the world needs

Think of the life-changers, from all eras and continents, who've made massive impacts on the world. Whether it was a scientist, an entrepreneur or an activist, they filled a need by doing something at which they excelled and they loved to do. It's not always about money, either: look at Mother Teresa.

My father loved his career, and he was quite good at it. Rounding out the three purpose definers mentioned above, did the world need electrical cords and light switches? Well, yes, but that's not life-changing. However, my father met other needs that the world desperately craves: appreciation, recognition, and leadership. He was a master at publicly praising his staff, and his managing skills led to record-breaking production. That's because his workers loved "Mr. Joe."

No, my father was never on the cover of a magazine. Some could say that he didn't make much of a difference in the big picture. But he did! He improved the lives of the people who worked for him. He gave them respect, firm leadership, and a sense of pride in a job well done.

We're not talking about curing Alzheimer's or inventing a perpetual-motion engine. Nor is it a matter of becoming rich and famous. It's about using your gifts and talents to become successful. When you do that, you can't help but shine. You'll be like a lighthouse in a dark storm.

Of course, if you can turn this purpose into a business, that would be awesome. Just think: you'd be doing what you enjoy full time, and it'd pay the bills. If you just said, "Yeah, right!" remember what we said in the last chapter about can't versus won't. If you want something badly enough, you'll figure out a way to make it a reality.

Your purpose can also be a favorite pastime. If you make the best cookies, bake away, my friend! Yes, it fills a need: who doesn't like cookies? Perhaps you love to ride motorcycles. You come alive when you hear that engine roar. You are also meeting the needs of the stores where you buy parts, or maybe you participate in fund-raising rides.

The point is that your energy and enthusiasm will be an inspiration to others. They don't even have to share your interest. They'll start to think, "Hmmm—if they're so happy, maybe I can be, too." Like a match, you'll be the spark in someone else's life. Then, they pursue their purpose, which lights more even matches. Wow! You can be the start of a powerful revolution!

YOUR LEGACY

When you include others in your journey, your relationships become stronger as you make memories together. You're building a bridge between generations. You give people something to look forward to, and the identity of being included.

For those of us interested in maintaining and teaching our families' traditions, you could make a video that tells the history of your ancestors. If your grandparents, aunts, and uncles are still alive, I implore you to record their stories. Trace the branches of your family tree, or assemble a cookbook of favorite recipes.

I heard about a unique tradition of one family that keeps the home fire burning brightly. By the time each person turns 50, they must have written their memories about growing up and how it made them who they are. They are also to include their hopes for the family in the future. Can you see how this is already a powerful heirloom? Imagine what it will be in a generation or two!

Your legacy isn't just one thing. It's every life that you touch. You never know how a small act of kindness can bring light to another. You're paying it forward, either in action or as a lesson.

A few times a year, I run into Tony BusStop. (No, that's not his real last name. Everyone calls him that because of the market he owned for decades was at a bus stop; the building is across the street from my grandparents' house that I now own.) Every time I see Mr. BusStop, he talks about how my grandfather poured the concrete step at the back door. He reminisces how my grandmother would send over pasta and huge sandwiches to him.

My grandparents simply did what they were good at, loved to do, and filled a need. They were simply being neighborly, yet someone still talks about it 60 years later. I love to hear these stories because of the pride for my grandparents' kindness and generosity, and because it inspires me to follow suit.

This is all about developing your legacy, and how your life will be remembered. What would you want people to say at your 90th birthday party? For one thing, I know that you don't want to be the only attendee! You can do many things now to make sure there are at least few glowing toasts in your honor.

Of course, the first place most of us start creating a legacy is with our families. Beyond that, there's a big world out there that could use your unique mix of skills. Following are two ideas. Consider inviting others to join you; it'll be even more meaningful.

• Mentoring

If you want to make a difference in children's lives, you could join an organization like Big Brothers. Don't forget that you can mentor your nieces, nephews and grandchildren, as well! There are also many opportunities in churches.

If you're successful in your career, you can guide others through their journeys. You might consider joining SCORE, which is a trusted resource for free business mentoring and education.

I met one of my mentors, Asterio, through his wife and daughter; we instantly became friends. A native Florentine, he told me to send him a daily email to help me to master the Italian language. He walked me through the linguistic subtleties that sometimes get lost in translation.

Over time, though, Asterio advised me on more than just grammar; he counseled me in all areas of life. He was often encouraging, but he wasn't shy about letting me know if I'd made a poor decision. I'm forever grateful for the time and love that he gave, which made me a better person.

You, too, can make a powerful impact on someone else's life just by being yourself. No, you don't have to hang up a sign to announce your availability as a mentor. Keep your eyes and ears open to the people around you, and share your experiences with them. You might be surprised that you get as much out of the relationship as they do.

• Volunteering

There are countless opportunities to pitch in with a group that cares about the issues that you do. Of course, you can always make a monetary donation, but I encourage you to show up to events when you can. That's where you feel their heartbeat, and you become more connected to your community while supporting an important cause.

Here are a few online resources to discover more altruistic opportunities:

VolunteerMatch.org
CreateTheGood.AARP.org
AllForGood.org

* * *

THE MATTERA LEGACY

Before my first trip to Italy, Uncle Johnny told me about our family there. He said, "Their generosity will change you." He was right.

Not just our family, but almost everyone we met was always giving more than expected. A shop owner in Florence would wrap up a trinket as if it were a diamond. People we'd just met in Rome invited us for dinner. A couple sitting beside us in a café was generous with their time and advice of the area.

Experiencing that in Italy made me appreciate even more how my grandparents carried that benevolent spirit to America. There was always cake and coffee on hand in case someone stopped by to visit. As soon as you walked in the door, they'd ask if you were hungry. Regardless of your answer, they'd make you "a little snack" which was more like a four-course meal! They would sometimes pretend to shake your hand, but they were actually slipping you some money.

My family's legacy boils down to one simple word: love.

Am I saying that we're all angels and choir boys? Heavens, no! As humans, we all make mistakes. My family even has a villain or two. However, the legacy that I choose to emphasize is that of love and hope. You have that choice, too, as you create *your* legacy!

Whether it's as simple as sharing zucchini from the garden or as brave as someone defending your character in your absence, it's done because of love. My continuing Italian lesson is to carry that spirit with me everywhere I go and to share it whenever possible.

You and I can be a light in this dark world, a lifeline of hope in a sea of despair. Take every chance you can to shine. In time, we can witness a rebirth—a Renaissance—in our world.

L'amore vince sempre. (Love always wins.)

—Italian proverb

CONCLUSION
BACI & ANTACID

Just like English speakers might sign a letter with "Hugs & kisses", Italians sweetly write *"Baci & abbracci."* (It's also a clothing company with headquarters in Milan.)

A while ago, my cousin Linda sent me an email and signed it *"Baci* & antacid." I thought she was being funny, changing *"abbracci"* (hugs) to "antacid". Considering the turmoil of the times, it would've been appropriately clever. Nope; blame it on autocorrect!

Doesn't that describe life? It's a dance between loving kisses and needing antacid. Our individual journeys harmonize like a symphony with high and low notes, and varied tempos. Even the sharps and flats have a place.

Each of us plays a part, making a breathtaking masterpiece. It'd be incomplete if you chose to put down your instrument. The audience of this world needs your unique blend of skills and personality. There are people out there who need to hear your song. They might not relate to my story, but yours will strike a chord.

Don't wait too long to start playing because no one is guaranteed tomorrow. If my parents' length of time on Earth is any indication of mine, I only have about a decade remaining. You may think that's morbid; I think it's sobering. Just before writing these words, I learned that my friend Frank Romano (mentioned in this book) passed away yesterday.

You've heard it time and again: life is short. Yes, it is. More importantly, what are you going to do about it? Challenge your fears and pursue the life you want. Do you want to make excuses, or do you want to make a difference?

My prayer is that you will ...

> ... *embrace your heritage, keeping alive the traditions that are most important to you,*
> ... *continue to learn from life's lessons and to move forward with optimism,*
> ... *recognize your worth and help others discover theirs,*
> ... *find your joy and purpose, and let your enthusiasm shine.*

If each of us did that, the ripple effect could transform this crazy world. Life will never be perfect, but it can be beautiful, meaningful, and brimming with hope.

"Life goes on..."

—Joe Mattera

"...it's up to us to make it extraordinary."

—Dawn Mattera

APPENDIX
LIFE, ITALIAN STYLE

ACTION STEPS TO GET STAMPS IN YOUR PASSPORT TO HOPE, HAPPINESS & YOUR PERSONAL RENAISSANCE

Chapter 1: *Insomma...* (So...)

1) Every night, before going to sleep, think of at least three things you're thankful for in your life. For extra credit, start your day that way, too.

2) What are your top three priorities? Each day, do something related to them—no matter how small.

3) What are some of your past victories? What attributes did you use to work through the situations? How can you apply them today?

Chapter 2: *Nessun Dorma* (No one sleeps)

1) What worries you?

2) What part(s) of it can you control? Take action!

3) Find quotes that inspire you to overcome fear and worry. Read them every morning.

Chapter 3: *Inferno* (Hell)

1) What are the things that energize you? Keep a list of them in the place you usually go when you're feeling down (the fridge door, the closet, the computer).

2) Another list to keep with the coffee list: what are activities that relax you?

3) First thing in the morning and before you sleep, think of all the sweet things in your life: friends, family, beauty, music, nature, etc. Remember that your thoughts ultimately determine your destiny, and you control what goes into your mind.

4) Repeat, repeat, repeat. Overcoming depression is not a weekend DIY project. We take small steps and repeat them daily until the black cloud no longer surrounds us.

Chapter 4: *Basta!* (Enough!)

1) Is there someone you can't imagine forgiving? Take a step toward grace. That might mean saying, every day, "I forgive (name)." You might write a letter to the offender—just don't send it! Remind yourself that forgiveness is to free you from the past and not justify his or her actions.

2) Do you need to ask to be forgiven by someone? Take the high road and contact that person…who may or may not be ready to talk. Hope for the best as you extend that olive branch. Be honest and humble, and don't use "but" in your apology.

3) Forgive yourself! We have all made mistakes, and we can learn from them. Today is when you draw a line in the sand between your past and your new self. Talk to yourself as you would to your best friend.

Chapter 5: When in Rome (habits)

1. Use the Blueprint for Better Behaviors from chapter five for that one habit you've talked about changing for a long time.

2. Be diligent about what you allow into your computer, um…mind. Decide what you'll do instead of watching the news. How will you redirect the conversation when some negative Nino starts complaining?

3. How do you want your life to be in ten years? What habit can you start today that'll be a key to achieving and keeping that level of success?

Chapter 6: *Paesan'!* (My friend!)

1) Call or text your dearest friend right now! Tell him or her why you appreciate your friendship.

2) Make a phone date with a long-distance friend.

3) Set a goal to sincerely compliment at least two people each day.

Chapter 7: *La famiglia* (family)

1) Discover the name day (*onomastico*) of your parents and grandparents. Tell the younger generation about them.

2) Attend a religious service. No, lightning won't strike! Even if you have a different faith than your family, go

with an open heart and find the commonalities in your beliefs.

3) Research the traditions of your family's past. Incorporate them into your daily life and certainly into the holidays.

Chapter 8: *Amore* (love)

1) Discover your Love Language and that of your partner (if applicable). You can find the free quiz on the author's website: www.5LoveLanguages.com

2) Every day, present your best self to the world. Not only will you feel more confident, it opens the door to meeting new people. Whether you're in a relationship or single, taking the time for self-care is part of the courting process. (Remember that continuing the things we did while dating our mate helps to keep the flame burning!)

3) Do something that you've never done before! If you're single, you will meet like-minded people. If you're half of a couple, new experiences strengthen your bonds of love.

Chapter 9: *La Bella Figura* (making a good impression)

1) Make a promise to yourself to only wear clothing that is appropriate for the occasion, fits well, and makes you feel great about yourself.

2) Be mindful of others: hold doors open, let someone merge onto the highway, and freely give sincere compliments.

Chapter 10: *Volare* (to fly)

1) Do something you've never done before that you've always wanted to.

2) Create playlists for different situations: relaxing, getting pumped up to exercise or tackle a task, hosting a dinner, and spending time with your *amore*.

3) Get involved with a cause that's near and dear to your heart.

Chapter 11: *Imparo ancora* (I'm still learning)

1) What are at least five successes that you've had in your life? What were the qualities (like perseverance or resourcefulness) that you used to achieve that success? Those are tools still in your toolbox! You now have an update to your brain's software about your true identity. "Run" that program every day.

2) What is something that you want to do in your life? Maybe you want to travel or write a book. It doesn't matter how old you are, your background or what's happening in the world! Do something today toward that goal.

3) Stop listening to your inner critic and start *speaking* to it! Every time a defeating thought enters your mind, challenge it, and then change it. If there's a grain of truth to that limiting belief, what can you do to improve? Then, do it!

Chapter 12: *Avanti!* (Go forth!)

1) Each night before you go to bed, write down all the things you need to do tomorrow. (Or do this first thing

in the morning.) What are the one or two most important things you can do that will have the greatest impact
on your priorities? Do them first!

2) Get pictures of rewards and/or images of how life will
be when you achieve different milestones. Post them
where you'll see them every day.

3) What are some "can't" statements that you tell yourself?
Are you really saying that you *won't*? Challenge those
excuses and remind yourself all the reasons why you
want to reach your goals.

Chapter 13: *Andiamo!* (Let's go!)

1) Define your purpose. It doesn't have to be just one
thing! Remember that it's something that you love to
do, you are good at, and that the world needs.

2) How do you want to be remembered? Do something
today that guests will talk about at your 90th birthday
party.

3) Commit to doing something every day to demonstrate
love. It could be as small as holding the door for a
stranger, or as grand as an over-the-top gift. Have fun
with it!

ENDNOTES

Chapter 2: *Nessun Dorma*

[1] Source: Chapman University *America's Top Fears* study https://www.chapman.edu/wilkinson/research-centers/babbie-center/survey-american-fears.aspx
[2] Arachibutyrophobia: the fear of peanut butter sticking to the roof of your mouth
[3] Andrews, A. (1991) *Storms of Perfection 1…in their own words.* Nashville, TN. Lightning Crown Publishers

Chapter 3: *Inferno*

[1] *Public Beliefs and Attitudes towards Depression in Italy: A National Survey* https://journals.plos.org/plosone/article?id=10.1371/journal.pone.0063806
[2] Chapman, G. (1992) *The 5 Love Languages: The Secret to Love That Lasts.* Chicago, IL. Northfield Publishing.

Chapter 7: *La famiglia*

[1] *The Importance of Family Dinners*, Columbia University, The National Center on Addiction and Substance Abuse, September 2012

Chapter 8: *Amore*

[1] Chapman, G. (1992). *The Five Love Languages: How to Express Heartfelt Commitment to Your Mate*. Chicago, IL. Northfield Publishing.
[2] Warren, H. and Brooks, J. (1953) *That's Amore*. Hollywood, CA. Capitol Records

Chapter 9: *La Bella Figura*

[1] *Journal of Experimental Social Psychology*, Vol 48, Issue 4, July 2012; Hajo Adam and Adam Galinsky, Northwestern University, Evanston, IL

Chapter 10: *Volare*

[1] https://www.happify.com/hd/science-of-happiness-infographic
[2] Dr. Yuna L. Ferguson and Dr. Kennon M. Sheldon. "Trying to be happier really can work: Two experimental studies." *The Journal of Positive Psychology*, Volume 8, Issue 1, 2013.
[3] Dr. Päivi-Sisko Eerola and Tuomas Eerola. "Extended Music Education Enhances The Quality Of School Life." Music Education Research 16.1 (2014): 88-104. ERIC. Web. 18 Nov. 2015.

ABOUT THE AUTHOR

Dawn Mattera is an author and speaker who has helped people for over 25 years achieve personal success and overcome challenges.

She has written articles and newsletters for international organizations, hosted and spoken at packed seminars and virtual events, and starred in monthly TV spots. Dawn holds a Bachelor's Degree in Electrical Engineering, a Diploma for the Italian Language, and is a Microsoft Office Master (but, would rather be a Jedi master).

In the span of just a few years, Dawn moved three times, was laid off twice, got divorced, and faced financial and psychological obstacles. With all that and a history of depression, one could imagine her checking into a local padded cell. However, she rose above the challenges, and she wants to encourage others do the same.

Dawn's mission is to help people realize their potentials, live their lives to the fullest, and make a difference in the world.

Born in New England, Dawn has lived in various states and in Florence, Italy. She and her life partner, Bob, have taken gladiator lessons in Rome and driven vintage FIAT 500s through Tuscany. They are still conducting research for the world's best *gelato*.

Read Dawn's global award-nominated first book:

La Bella Figura: Italian Secrets about Being Happy, Healthy and Hot!

Do you want to be happy, healthy and hot?
La bella figura has a figurative and literal translation. In this book, you'll learn the Italian secrets for both: looking, feeling and being your best.

We'll journey through the calendar with each month highlighting a unique aspect of the Italian culture and how we can apply it to our lives.

Each chapter also includes a recipe or two of Italian favorites with the fat and calories slashed. You'll also see some twists on traditional favorites.

Wonderful Insight to Living a Happy, Healthy Life!!
Ms. Mattera celebrates her Italian ancestry in this fun, well written book. She takes a typical year - month by month - and explains the celebrations and traditions of Italy. She also takes several Italian recipes, normally higher in calories, and gives tips on how to lighten them up. The photographs are breathtaking. I would definitely recommend this uplifting book.

—Annie M

Entertainingly delicious!
Ms. Mattera has written an entertainingly delicious cookbook that becomes a gift for your palate.

—Stephen I

Page 30 of *La Bella Figura* has an Italian proverb about "find a friend, find a treasure". I'd change the quote to say, "He who finds this book, finds a treasure."

—Carol H

Available in print and eBook versions

Keep adding stamps to your Passport to Hope, Happiness and Your Personal Renaissance!

Stay inspired to:

- Live a life of passion and purpose
- Develop a sense of Italian style
- Travel off the beaten path

DawnMattera.com

Get a free guide: Five Ways to Boost Your Happiness in Five Minutes…Italian Style!

Bring Dawn to Your Next Event

Do you want a dynamic and enthusiastic speaker for your group? Dawn is available to speak to your group, in person or online. Topics can be customized for your organization and include:

- Overcoming challenges (including depression, fears and excuses)
- The importance of family heritage and traditions, and how to keep them alive
- Authentic and unique travel adventures

ABOUT THE PUBLISHER

Is there a book inside you? Sharing your unique story can change lives!

Publishing a book can be confusing and costly, but not if you find the right team.

Author Academy has a proven system to help you write, publish and promote your book. Learn about the 18 possible streams of income!

AAE

For more information, and to watch a FREE webinar about turning your idea into income, go to:

https://tinyurl.com/DawnAlba

CPSIA information can be obtained
at www.ICGtesting.com
Printed in the USA
BVHW072153221120
593941BV00001B/144